C000183244

With a judicious and knowledgea
ary literature, Haykin has produc
of the life of St Patrick. Readers
dence produced that points to Patrick's strong commitment to
missions, evangelism and Scripture.

D. H. Williams
Professor of Patristics and Historical Theology,
Baylor University, Waco, Texas

Living as we do in a time of moral collapse and cultural destruction, it is remarkably encouraging to be able to look back almost
1,600 years to a man whom God used to begin a renewal of
Christianity. In these pages Michael Haykin introduces to
us Patrick, whom the Lord sent as his missionary to Ireland.
Originally enslaved and then converted there, this man, after
being trained in Britain, was led back for service in the island
on the western edge of Europe.

An outline of the contemporary context and of his life is followed by a summary of his theology, which was based solidly on
the Bible and committed among other aspects to the reality of
the Trinity and the balance in daily piety of the Word and the
Spirit. Patrick's effective ministry led in time to re-evangelism in
other countries and a substantial developing of the church. To
read this account is to fill us with thankfulness for the Lord's
work in history and with hopefulness for perhaps a similar work
in another era of lost-ness.

Edward Donnelly
Principal, Reformed Theological College,
Belfast, Northern Ireland

There is one theme that stands out from this beautifully detailed portrait in miniature: Patrick's missionary zeal was grounded in a deep Trinitarian faith. Patrick's *Confession* and his life ever show us how the Trinity should be at the heart of our thought and prayer. And thus all Christians will benefit from learning more about this mighty figure in the great cloud of witnesses.

Lewis Ayres
Professor of Historical Theology, Durham University,
Durham, England

Sometimes the historical figure outshines the legend. By sifting through reliable sources, Michael Haykin paints a compelling portrait of this bibliocentric bishop and earnest evangelist. The dedicated missionary and thoughtful theologian that emerges belongs to the gospel-loving global church and not just the Emerald Isle. The persistent Patrick, a diligent minister of the Word and Spirit, deserves to be commemorated far more than once each year.

Paul Hartog
Adjunct Faculty of Biblical Studies, Faith Baptist Bible College
and Theological Seminary, Ankeny, Iowa

What fires a man to be a missionary in a country where he has been a slave? Michael Haykin's book is a fine balance between a biography of an extraordinary servant of Jesus Christ and an explanation of the beliefs that sustained Patrick. Patrick was a man whose situation is very different from ours and whose beliefs differ from ours at points too, and Haykin is especially helpful in exemplifying how we as today's Evangelicals can learn from someone so different and yet also close kin.

Michael Ovey
Principal, Oak Hill Theological College, London

EARLY CHURCH FATHERS

PATRICK OF IRELAND

His Life and Impact

MICHAEL A. G. HAYKIN

WITH AARON MATHERLY AND SHAWN J. WILHITE

Series editor:

Michael A. G. Haykin

Scripture quotations are from *The Holy Bible, English Standard Version*, copyright © 2001 by Crossway Bibles, a division of Good News Publishers. Used by permission. All rights reserved. ESV Text Edition: 2007.

Michael A. G. Haykin is Professor of Church History and Biblical Spirituality at the Southern Baptist Theological Seminary, Louisville, Kentucky where he is also Director of the Andrew Fuller Center for Baptist Studies. He has written several books and is the series editor of the Early Church Fathers series.

Copyright © Michael A. G. Haykin 2014

Michael A. G. Haykin has asserted his right under the Copyright, Designs and Patents Act, 1988, to be identified as Author of this work.

paperback ISBN 978-1-78191-303-1
epub ISBN 978-1-78191-373-4
Mobi ISBN 978-1-78191-374-1

First published in 2014
by
Christian Focus Publications Ltd,
Geanies House, Fearn, Ross-shire
IV20 1TW, Scotland
www.christianfocus.com

A CIP catalogue record for this book is available from the British Library.

Cover artwork illustrator: Hélène Grondines
Cover designer: Daniel van Straaten

Printed by Bell and Bain, Glasgow

All rights reserved. No part of this publication may be reproduced, stored in a retrieval system, or transmitted, in any form, by any means, electronic, mechanical, photocopying, recording or otherwise without the prior permission of the publisher or a license permitting restricted copying. In the U.K. such licenses are issued by the Copyright Licensing Agency, Saffron House, 6-10 Kirby Street, London, EC1 8TS www.cla.co.uk.

CONTENTS

DEDICATION

In memory of my beloved Irish mother,
Teresa Veronica O'Gorman Haykin (1933–1976):
'Precious in the sight of the Lord is the death of his saints.'

On reading the Church Fathers

By common definition, the Church Fathers are those early
Christian authors who wrote between the close of the first
century, right after the death of the last of the apostles, namely
the apostle John, and the middle of the eighth century. In other
words, those figures who were active in the life of the church
between Ignatius of Antioch and Clement of Rome, who
penned writings at the very beginning of the second century,
and the Venerable Bede and John of Damascus, who stood at
the close of antiquity and the onset of the Middle Ages. Far
too many Evangelicals in the modern day know next to nothing
about these figures. I will never forget being asked to give a mini-
history conference at a church in southern Ontario. I suggested
three talks on three figures from Latin-speaking North Africa:
Perpetua, Cyprian, and Augustine. The leadership of the church
came back to me seeking a different set of names, since they
had never heard of the first two figures, and while they had
heard of the third name, the famous bishop of Hippo Regius,
they really knew nothing about him. I gave them another list of

post-Reformation figures for the mini-conference, but privately thought that not knowing anything about these figures was possibly a very good reason to have a conference on them! I suspect that such ignorance is quite widespread among those who call themselves Evangelicals — hence the importance of this small series of studies on a select number of Church Fathers, to educate and inform God's people about their forebears in the faith.

Past appreciation for the Fathers

How different is the modern situation from the past, when many of our Evangelical and Reformed forebears knew and treasured the writings of the ancient church. The French Reformer John Calvin, for example, was ever a keen student of the Church Fathers. He did not always agree with them, even when it came to one of his favorite authors, namely, Augustine. But he was deeply aware of the value of knowing their thought and drawing upon the riches of their written works for elucidating the Christian faith in his own day. And in the seventeenth century, the Puritan theologian John Owen, rightly called the 'Calvin of England' by some of his contemporaries, was not slow to turn to the experience of the one he called 'holy Austin,' namely Augustine, to provide him with a pattern of God the Holy Spirit's work in conversion.

Yet again, when the Particular Baptist John Gill was faced with the anti-Trinitarianism of the Deist movement in the early eighteenth century, and other Protestant bodies — for instance, the English Presbyterians, the General Baptists, and large tracts of Anglicanism — were unable to retain a firm grasp on this utterly vital biblical doctrine, Gill turned to the Fathers to help him elucidate the biblical teaching regarding the blessed Trinity. Gill's example in this regard influenced other Baptists such as John Sutcliff, pastor of the Baptist cause in Olney, where John Newton also ministered. Sutcliff was so impressed by the *Letter to Diognetus*, which he wrongly supposed to have been written by Justin Martyr, that he translated it for *The Biblical Magazine*, a Calvinistic publication with a small circulation. He sent it to the editor of this periodical with the commendation that this second-century work is 'one of the most valuable pieces of ecclesiastical antiquity.'

One final caveat

One final word about the Fathers recommended in this small series of essays. The Fathers are not Scripture. They are senior conversation partners about Scripture and its meaning. We listen to them respectfully, but are not afraid to disagree when they err. As the Reformers rightly argued, the writings of the Fathers must be subject to Scripture. John Jewel, the Anglican apologist, put it well when he stated in 1562:

> But what say we of the fathers, Augustine, Ambrose, Jerome, Cyprian, etc.? What shall we think of them, or what account may we make of them? They be interpreters of the word of God. They were learned men, and learned fathers; the instruments of the mercy of God, and vessels full of grace. We despise them not, we read them, we reverence them, and give thanks unto God for them. They were witnesses unto the truth, they were worthy pillars and ornaments in the church of God. Yet may they not be compared with the word of God. We may not build upon them: we may not make them the foundation and warrant of our conscience: we may not put our trust in them. Our trust is in the name of the Lord.

Michael A. G. Haykin
The Southern Baptist Theological Seminary
Louisville, Kentucky, U.S.A.

A CHRONOLOGY OF PATRICK

Around A.D. 390   Birth of Patrick

406   Patrick taken captive by Irish raiders

Winter, 406–407   Rhine river freezes, enabling Germanic warriors to cross over and ravage the Roman territories of Gaul and Hispania

411   Death of Constantine III

412   Patrick returns to Britain

Late 410s–420s   Patrick receives theological training in Britain

429	Germanus, bishop of Auxerre, sent to ward off Pelagianism in Britain
Around 430–460	Patrick's ministry in Ireland
Around 460	Death of St Patrick
521–597	Columba, Irish abbot and missionary
529	Council of Orange
543–615	Columbanus, Irish missionary
604/609	Death of Augustine of Canterbury
651	Death of Aidan, Irish monk and missionary
652	Cummian, abbot of Durrow, breaks silence about Patrick
fl.690	Tírechán, biographer of St Patrick (cf. *Book of Armagh*)
fl.697	Muirchú, biographer of St Patrick (cf. *Book of Armagh*)
807	Composition of the *Book of Armagh*
1905	First authoritative biography of Patrick, written by J.B. Bury

PREFACE

Among the very few names of Christian believers from the late third- or early fourth-century Roman province of Britannia (henceforth called Britain) that have come down to us are four inhabitants of Durobrivae (now Water Newton in Cambridgeshire). Established at the spot where Ermine Street crosses the River Nene, Durobrivae had begun as a garrison fort, but in time it became one of the wealthiest towns of the province, its wealth accruing from large-scale pottery and mosaic industries. In 1975, a cache of Christian silver was found within the remains of this Roman town that has been identified as having been used for worship, and as such is the oldest collection of liturgical vessels from the Roman Empire. A number of the pieces are stamped with the familiar Christian chi-rho symbol—chi and rho are the first two letters (ΧΡ) of the word Christ in Greek, ΧΡΙΣΤΟΣ (*Christos*), and were combined thus:

The names of four Christians associated with the cache are also discernible on some of the vessels: Publianus, Iamcilla, Innocentia and Viventia—one man and three women. Who were these fourth-century believers? How had they come to Christ? What was their witness? They may well have been part of a Christian community composed mostly of industrial workers from the potteries, though these four individuals must have been wealthy enough to have donated these silver vessels to the church.[1] Beyond these sparse facts, we can only speculate. If these four Christians have come down to us as mere names, there is a Christian from this province, born in the fourth century, who is far more than such: Patricius, or as we know him today, Patrick.

Unlike the four Christians from Durobrivae, Patrick has left two sources from his own hand that enable a book like this about his life and his theology to be written: his *Confession*, written at the very close of his life,[2] and a blistering letter to a Romano-British chieftain by the name of Coroticus, who, in a raid on Ireland, had killed a number of newly-baptized

1.   R.P.C. Hanson, *The Life and Writings of the Historical Saint Patrick* (New York, NY: The Seabury Press, 1983), pp. 9-10; Peter Salway, *The Oxford Illustrated History of Roman Britain* (Oxford/New York, NY: Oxford University Press, 1993), pp. 514-15; Malcolm Lambert, *Christians and Pagans: The Conversion of Britain from Alban to Bede* (New Haven/London: Yale University Press, 2010), pp. 22-23. Sam Moorhead and David Stuttard believe there is evidence of pagan influence in this silver collection—see their *The Romans Who Shaped Britain* (London: Thames & Hudson, 2012), p. 243.

2.   See his reference to 'my old age' (*senectute mea*) in *Confession* 10 and his statement in *Confession* 62: 'This is my confession before I die' (trans. Ludwig Bieler, *The Works of St Patrick, St Secundinus: Hymn on St Patrick* [Ancient Christian Writers, no.17; 1953 ed.; repr. New York/Ramsey, New Jersey: Paulist Press, n.d.], p. 40). Unless otherwise indicated, the translation of Patrick's works that I have used is this one by Bieler. For the Latin, I have used Richard P.C. Hanson and Cécile Blanc, *Saint Patrick: Confession et Lettre à Coroticus* (Sources Chrétiennes, no. 249; Paris: Les Éditions du Cerf, 1978), which E.A. Thompson has praised as 'a model introduction to St Patrick and his two surviving works' ('Reviews', *Britannia*, 11 [1980], p. 438). I have occasionally made my own translation of sections of Patrick's texts or modified Bieler's translation. Where I have done so, this has been clearly indicated.

Christians and enslaved others.[3] To be sure, other texts have come down to us purportedly from Patrick, but none as extensive as the two texts just mentioned and none with as firm a claim to authenticity as these two.[4]

As R.P.C. Hanson (1916–1988) – one-time Bishop of Clogher in the Church of Ireland and a noted expert on the Early Church – has observed, history has been enormously generous to Patrick.[5] Of the hundred or more saints whose memory was celebrated on a specific day by the medieval Roman Catholic Church, St Patrick's day is one of the very few to survive in the modern calendar. The green of Ireland is remembered every year around the world on March 17 and Patrick is everywhere the symbol of Irishness.[6] And from the Middle Ages onwards, his mission to Ireland was depicted as one astounding miracle after another. For example, Jocelin of Furness (fl.1175–1214), the English Cistercian hagiographer, explained the absence of snakes in Ireland to be the result of Patrick's destruction of them all on the peak of Croagh Patrick (St Patrick's Mountain) in County Mayo.[7] Jocelin also tells us that Patrick as an infant was baptized by a blind priest who got the water for the baptism by causing Patrick to make the sign of the cross over some earth, from which a well of water immediately issued. The water cured the priest of his blindness and enabled him, though illiterate, to read the rite of baptism. According to other miracles ascribed to Patrick, he was able to pass through doors, like the risen Christ, and could

---

3.   The identity of Coroticus is discussed more on p. 52.

4.   For discussion of these sources, see Bieler, *The Works of St Patrick*, pp. 8-14 and Hanson, *Life and Writings of the Historical Saint Patrick*, pp. 12-18. See also the discussion of sources for the life of Patrick in Chapter 1.

5.   *Life and Writings of the Historical Saint Patrick*, p. 1.

6.   For the rise of St Patrick's Day, see Bridget McCormack, *Perceptions of St Patrick in Eighteenth-Century Ireland* (Dublin: Four Courts Press, 2000), pp. 69-84.

7.   Daniel Ogden, *Dragons, Serpents, & Slayers in the Classical and Early Christian Worlds. A Sourcebook* (Oxford/New York: Oxford University Press, 2013), p, 248. See also Katharine Scherman, *The Flowering of Ireland: Saints, Scholars and Kings* (Boston/Toronto: Little, Brown and Co., 1981), pp. 93-4.

turn butter into honey.[8] Such 'miracles' indeed elevated Patrick
to iconic status, but the true measure and mettle of the man was
obscured. As this book will argue, Patrick was indeed a remarkable man, but it was not because of such 'absurd wonders'.[9] His
life was indeed wonder-full, but it was wonderful in the way the
apostle Paul's was: suffering and giving his all for the sake of the
gospel of the Lord he loved, the Lord Jesus.[10]

This author – of Irish descent and therefore an heir, albeit distantly, of those Irish men and women converted under
Patrick's preaching – has sought to capture something of the
remarkable quality of Patrick's life and faith. The bibliography
of scholarship on Patrick is an extensive one.[11] Alan Macquarrie
has put it well: 'Of all the early saints of the British Isles, none
has aroused greater controversy or generated a more voluminous
literature than has St Patrick.'[12] This work makes no claim to
ground-breaking scholarship in Patrician studies, but it does
seek to elucidate the theology of the man in a way that will help
Evangelical Christians, far too often uninterested in the history
of the ancient church, appreciate a fellow believer from that era.

The first chapter sets Patrick in the flow of history, outlines his
life, and deals with some key questions that surround his life and
ministry. Chapter 2 focuses on his Trinitarianism, utterly foundational to the theology of the ancient church and clearly foundational to the thought of Patrick, but all too frequently marginal
in the life of contemporary Evangelical and Reformed believers.
The next chapter develops Patrick's thinking about the missionary

8.   Charles H.H. Wright, 'Introduction' to his *The Writings of Patrick, The Apostle of Ire-
     land* (Christian Classics Series, no.VI; London: Religious Tract Society, n.d.), p. 16.

9.   Wright, 'Introduction' to his *Writings of Patrick*, pp. 16-17.

10. On Patrick's love for God, see *Confession* pp. 16, 36, 44, 59.

11. For some of this bibliography, see 'Further Reading' at the close of this book.

12. Alan Macquarrie, 'St Patrick of Ireland' in his *The Saints of Scotland: Essays in Scot-
     tish Church History A.D. 450–1093* (Edinburgh: John Donald Publishers, 1997),
     p. 31. With regard to the numerous writers about Patrick, E.A. Thompson has
     made the astute observation that among them is 'a lunatic fringe as massive as the
     Mountains of Mourne' in Ulster! See his 'Reviews', p. 439.

task of the church, of which he stands as a splendid exemplar. The final chapter looks at the balance of Word and Spirit in Patrick's thinking and experience, a topic of keen debate today.[13] Not every knot of interpretation with regard to Patrick's life and ministry is treated in this book – for example, I do not probe Patrick's relationship to Palladius, who is said to have gone to Ireland as a missionary bishop just before Patrick – for this essay is essentially an exercise in *ressourcement* or the recovery of a theology and a piety of the past that can be of help to believers in the present.

Acknowledgments

I owe a deep debt of gratitude to two of my students: Aaron Matherly, finishing his MDiv. at The Southern Baptist Theological Seminary, who wrote some portions of chapter 1 and an initial draft of some paragraphs in chapter 4, as well as the section on 'Further Reading'; and Shawn J. Wilhite, doing a doctorate in New Testament studies at Southern Seminary, who helped me finish the final draft of two of the sections of chapter 4 and also most helpfully did a copy edit on the entire manuscript. I wish to thank Daniel Williams for his careful reading of the manuscript and pointing out some errors. I am also thankful for a helpful conversation with Billy Fennell of Louisville, KY, about Patrick's dates and for the help given by Whitney Motley, Interlibrary Loan Coordinator in the James P. Boyce Centennial Library at Southern Seminary, and Christi Osterday, Circulation Coordinator in the same library.

Michael A.G. Haykin
Dundas, Ontario
November 5, 2013.

---

13. As I write these words, the 'Strange Fire' conference held October 16–18, 2013, at Grace Community Church in Southern California, has concluded within the past month. At this conference's heart was the age-old question of the relationship between the Holy Spirit and the Scriptures he has infallibly inspired. And judging by the mini-brouhaha that resulted from this conference via various forms of social media, this question is a key one for Evangelicals today.

'I AM PATRICK':
The Life and Historical Context of Patrick

The Roman Imperium and Britain

When Patrick was born in the late fourth century A.D., the Romans had been in Britain for roughly 350 years. In the first fifty years or so of Roman rule, there had been stiff resistance to the Romans in three regions in particular: by the Celtic tribes in what would become Wales; by Boudicca (d. 60/61), the Queen of the Iceni, inhabitants of present-day East Anglia, who led a massive rebellion; and by the Brigantes in northern Britain.[1] But after the suppression of the revolt of Boudicca, which came close to ending Roman rule in Britain, southern Britain was pacified. The northern Celts, the Brigantes, were suppressed in the 70s. As for what is now Scotland, Caledonia to the Romans, its conquest also provided major challenges to the invader. Despite a victory over the Caledonian tribes at Mons Graupius in north-east Scotland in 83,[2] the Romans eventually abandoned Scotland. For a period of time, between 142 and

---

1.   Guy de la Bédoyère, *Roman Britain: A New History* (New York: Thames & Hudson, 2006), pp. 31-44. On Boudicca, see the overview by T.W. Potter, 'Boudica (*d. AD* 60/61)', *Oxford Dictionary of National Biography*, Oxford University Press, 2004 (http://www.oxforddnb.com.libaccess.lib.mcmaster.ca/view/article/2732, accessed April 23, 2013).

2.   For the main literary description of this key engagement, see Tacitus, *Agricola* 29–37. For a modern discussion of the battle, see Nic Fields, *Rome's Northern Frontier A.D. 70–235* (Oxford: Osprey Publishing, 2005), pp. 8-10.

164, they occupied southern Scotland and built a defensive wall, the Antonine Wall, which ran across the Forth-Clyde isthmus. Eventually, though, the northern frontier was established at Hadrian's Wall in what is now northern England.[3]

South of Hadrian's Wall, the Romans crisscrossed the land with a network of roads and urban centres of importance, such as Ebracum (York), Glevum (Gloucester) and Londinium (London), were developed. Before the Roman conquest of Britannia, although the Britons had hill-forts and one or two places like Calleva (Silchester) that had certain features in common with Roman towns (*oppida*), there was no real urban culture where settlements had 'permanent architecture, clearly defined commercial and administrative areas, or residential zones'.[4] Roman rule also led to lavish villas dotting the countryside, built by the Romano-British upper class. Among these wealthy Britons, there grew to be an appreciation of and desire for Roman culture, and they subsequently sought to ensure that their children received a proper Roman education. The Roman historian Tacitus (*c.*56–*c.*120) depicts this eagerness of the British upper classes to acquire Roman culture in a famous text from his biography of Gnaeus Julius Agricola (40–93), the Roman general who was instrumental in extending Roman rule throughout northern Britain and who also happened to be Tacitus's father-in-law:

> [Agricola] educated the sons of the [British] chiefs in the liberal arts. ... The result was that instead of loathing the Latin language they became eager to speak it effectively. In the same way, our national dress came into favour and the toga was everywhere to be seen.[5]

---

3.   For an excellent study of the wall, see Nic Fields, *Hadrian's Wall* A.D. *122–410* (Oxford: Osprey Publishing, 2003).

4.   De la Bédoyère, *Roman Britain*, pp. 131-2.

5.   *Agricola* 21, trans. H. Mattingly and revised S.A. Handford, *Tacitus: The Agricola and the Germania* (Harmondsworth, Middlesex: Penguin Books Ltd., 1970), pp. 72-3. For a brief review of Agricola's career in Britannia, see De la Bédoyère, *Roman Britain*, pp. 42-7. See also the extremely helpful overview by Malcolm Todd, 'Julius Agricola, Gnaeus (A.D. 40–93)', *Oxford Dictionary of National Biography*, Oxford University Press, 2004 (http://www.oxforddnb.com.libaccess.lib.mcmaster.ca/view/article/48290, accessed April 23, 2013).

It is not surprising that the members of this social stratum became genuinely bilingual, conversant in both their native British and the Latin of their rulers. On the other hand, the lower classes, especially those in rural areas probably knew little, if any, Latin.[6] The ability of Patrick to write in Latin, albeit imperfectly as we shall see, is a clue to his social origins: he was from the upper class of Romano-British society.[7]

At the close of the fourth century, however, the comfortable world of the Romanized British upper class was about to be shattered, never to be restored. During the last quarter of that century the Empire had suffered a number of severe body blows which would precipitate the total collapse of imperial rule in the West in the following century. Those momentous events were naturally not without impact on Roman Britain. During the winter of 406–407, the Rhine river, the natural northern frontier of the Western Roman Empire, froze to such an extent that a large number of Germanic warriors were able to cross over to ravage the Roman territories of Gaul and Hispania. They were never driven out. The following summer, Constantine III (d. 411), a usurper who had been elevated to imperial power by the army in Britain, crossed the Channel, ostensibly to repel the barbarians. The legions never returned.

In the decades that followed, the British sought to organize their own defence against Saxon raiders from the east and hit-and-run attacks by Irish pirates from the west. But with the departure of the legions, economic and cultural decay started to set in. Towns began to be deserted and the lavish villas of the upper classes abandoned. The monetary system began to suffer decay

6.   Kenneth Jackson, *Language and History in Early Britain* (Edinburgh: Edinburgh University Press, 1953), pp. 97-106.

7.   See the discussion of Patrick's social background by R.P.C. Hanson, *The Life and Writings of the Historical Saint Patrick* (New York, NY: The Seabury Press, 1983), pp. 4-5; E.A. Thompson, *Who Was Saint Patrick?* (Woodbridge, Suffolk: The Boydell Press, 1985), pp. 40-1; Máire B. de Paor, *Patrick: The Pilgrim Apostle of Ireland* (New York, NY: Regan Books, 1998), pp. 26-8.

and the Roman system of education also probably collapsed.[8] But what did not collapse or leave with the Roman legions was the Christian witness in the archipelago.

The British church[9]

While Patrick's writings constitute some of the earliest literary evidence from an actual member of the British church, there is written testimony going back to the second century regarding the presence of Christianity in the British Isles. In the 190s the North African author Tertullian (fl.190–220), for instance, states in his *Against the Jews* that Christianity had spread so far it had reached Britain and had gone beyond the Antonine Wall. In answer to his question, 'In whom else have all the nations believed, than in the Christ who has already come?' he states that even 'places in Britain ..., though inaccessible to the Romans, have yielded to Christ.'[10] It may well be the case, as Roger Pearse has suggested, that this reference to the province of Britannia is due to its reputation for being remote,[11] though a reference a few years later by the learned Alexandrian exegete Origen (c. 185–253/254) to Christianity's presence in remote Britannia seems to indicate that Tertullian's knowledge, so far as it goes, is accurate. Origen was aware that the Christian faith had secured adherents in Britain by his day, for he asked, 'when ever did the land of Britain agree on the worship of one god before the arrival of Christ?' By the late second century/early third century, then, 'British Christianity was sufficiently well-founded and its membership sufficiently large that Christians in North Africa and Alexandria' knew of its

---

8.   Hanson, *Life and Writings of the Historical Saint Patrick*, p. 7.

9.   For an excellent study of the church in Roman Britain, see David Petts, *Christianity in Roman Britain* (Stroud, Gloucestershire/Charleston, SC: Tempus Publishing, 2003).

10. *Against the Jews* 7. See also Joseph F. Kelly, 'The Origins of Christianity in Britain: The Literary Evidence' (Unpublished paper, May, 1983), pp. 4-5.

11. See his web-page 'Adversus Judaeos (Against the Jews)' at his www.tertullian.org (accessed April 23, 2013).

existence.[12] How Christianity first came to the shores of Britain is impossible to determine. Patristic scholar W.H.C. Frend plausibly suggested that it was brought there by merchants or by soldiers garrisoned in Britain.[13] Douglas Dales believes Jewish Christian traders in London to be the most likely bearers of the faith, for one of the early martyrs in Britain was a Christian with the Jewish name of Aaron.[14] But up until the fourth century very little is known with certainty, in the way of either literary or archaeological evidence, about Christianity in Britain. With the fourth century, however, there appear a number of statements about the British church and its bishops by contemporary authors on the continent.[15] Two that are of some import are those made by Athanasius of Alexandria (c. 299–373) and Hilary of Poitiers (c. 300–c. 368) to the effect that the British church had fully assented to the Nicene Creed and its condemnation of the fourth-century heresy, Arianism, which denied the full deity of the Lord Jesus and the Holy Spirit.[16] As we shall see, a significant part of Patrick's spiritual bequest to the Celts in Ireland will be a doctrine of the Trinity that is in full accord with that of the Nicene Creed.

The Nicene Creed: The original Nicene Creed, issued at the Council of Nicaea in 325, did not contain a paragraph on the Holy Spirit. To rectify this lacuna, a new creed, which is also commonly called the Nicene Creed, was issued at the Council of Constantinople in 381. It runs as follows:

12. Kelly, 'Origins of Christianity in Britain', p. 5. cf. Henry Chadwick, *The Early Church* (Rev. ed.; London: Penguin Books, 1993), p. 63, who believes that it was not until the middle of the third century that Christianity was securely established.

13. 'Romano-British Christianity and the West: Comparison and Contrast' in Susan M. Pearce, ed., *The Early Church in Western Britain and Ireland* (Oxford: B.A.R. [British Archaeological Reports], 1982), p. 6.

14. *Light to the Isles. A study of missionary theology in Celtic and early Anglo-Saxon Britain* (Cambridge: Lutterworth Press, 1997), p. 27. For the brief account of his death, see Bede, *Ecclesiastical History* 1.7.

15. See Dales, *Light to the Isles*, pp. 27-8.

16. Athanasius, *Letter to the Emperor Jovian* 2; Hilary, *On Synods* 1.

> We believe in one God, the Father Almighty, Maker of heaven and earth, and of all things visible and invisible.
>
> And we believe in one Lord Jesus Christ, the only-begotten Son of God, eternally begotten from the Father; Light from Light, true God from true God; begotten, not made, of one being with the Father; by whom all things were made. Who, for us men and for our salvation, came down from heaven, and was incarnate by the Holy Spirit and the Virgin Mary, and was made man. For our sake, he was crucified under Pontius Pilate; He suffered and was buried; and on the third day he rose again, according to the Scriptures; and ascended into heaven, and sits on the right hand of the Father; and he shall come again, with glory, to judge the living and the dead; whose kingdom shall have no end.
>
> And we believe in the Holy Spirit, the Lord and Giver of Life, who proceeds from the Father, who with the Father and the Son together is worshipped and glorified, who spoke by the prophets.
>
> And we believe in one, holy, catholic and apostolic Church; we acknowledge one baptism for the remission of sins; and we look for the resurrection of the dead, and the life of the world to come. Amen.

Archaeological evidence from third- and fourth-century Britain also confirms a growing acceptance of Christianity by the upper classes, a movement that was parallel to what was happening in the rest of the Empire.[17] Archaeologists have uncovered Christian places of worship dating to the fourth and fifth centuries, for example. One of the most interesting of these is at Lullingstone in Kent. Among a number of wealthy villas in the valley of the River Darent has been found a villa that contained at one point a Christian house-church. This villa was built towards the

17. For a discussion of the evidence for the existence of Christianity in Britain up to and including the fourth century, R.P.C. Hanson, *Saint Patrick: His Origins and Career* (Oxford: Clarendon Press, 1968), pp. 30-4; Charles Thomas, *Christianity in Roman Britain to A.D. 500* (London: Batsford Academic and Educational Ltd., 1981); Kelly, 'Origins', pp. 5-9; Philip Freeman, *St Patrick of Ireland. A Biography* (New York, NY: Simon & Schuster, 2004), pp. 59-60.

close of the first century, and in the following century it was substantially expanded by a man who clearly possessed considerable wealth. At the beginning of the third century, however, the villa was suddenly deserted and it lay derelict for the next fifty years or so. During much of this time the empire experienced major political and military challenges, and the dereliction of the villa may well have had something to do with these events. It was re-occupied in the final twenty-five years of that century, possibly during the time when the Emperor Diocletian was able to bring the Empire back from the brink of disaster (240–316). By 360–370, the owner was a Christian, and he deliberately adapted a wing of the villa to Christian worship. The remains of paintings on the walls of one of the rooms in this wing, now in the British Museum, have been reconstructed enough for us to identify a large chi-rho symbol surrounded by a wreath. It has also been possible to reconstruct a series of seven four-feet tall figures that adorned the west wall of this worship centre: each of the figures is clothed in beautiful, brightly coloured garments, and standing in the posture of prayer.[18] This was no doubt an estate chapel, available for the Christians who worked on the villa's property as well as for the people who lived in the villa.[19]

Then, by the turn of the fifth century we encounter for the first time prominent British churchmen: men such as Pelagius (375/380–423/429), whose perspective on the Christian faith brought about a far-ranging controversy with that colossal thinker of antiquity, Augustine (354–430); and Faustus (c.408–c.490), bishop of Riez and a well-known preacher in Gaul.[20]

---

18. See H.H. Scullard, *Roman Britain, Outpost of the Empire* (London: Thames and Hudson, 1979), pp. 119-21, 166-8; Roger J.A. Wilson, *A Guide to the Roman Remains in Britain* (London: Constable and Company Ltd., 1975), pp. 52-3; Petts, *Christianity in Roman Britain*, pp. 79-81.

19. Hanson, *Life and Writings of the Historical Saint Patrick*, pp. 8-9; Chadwick, *Early Church*, p. 63.

20. For Faustus, see J.G. Cazenove, 'Faustus (11)' in *A Dictionary of Christian Biography*, eds. William Smith and Henry Wace (London: John Murray, 1880), II, pp. 467-70; Hanson, *Saint Patrick: His Origins and Career*, pp. 63-5.

Sources for the life of Patrick

R.P.C. Hanson has rightly noted that a doctoral thesis could be written simply on the history of scholarship about Patrick, for there are a number of aspects about his life that are not at all clear-cut.[21] There is no agreement, for example, about the date of his birth or the location of his childhood home, or about the place of his captivity in Ireland or whether or not he had formal theological education; nor is there any agreement about the dates of his ministry in Ireland. Part of the disparity of opinion among scholars who have written about Patrick can be attributed to the sources used in reconstructing his biography. Given the lack of any archeological evidence in Ireland dating to the time of Patrick, historians must rely on written documents.[22] Hanson identifies three classes of literary sources that give us information about Patrick: works written by Patrick or attributed to him, later lives of Patrick, and references to Patrick in the Irish *Annals*.[23] The first class consists of the *Confession* and the *Letter to the Soldiers of Coroticus*; both of these were clearly written by Patrick.[24] However, the authenticity of other poems and sayings that have been attributed to Patrick, such as the *Hymn of St Secundinus*, is far from certain. The second class includes later biographies of Patrick that first appear in seventh-century Ireland, some 200 years removed from Patrick's own life. Prominent among these are writings found in the Irish *Book of Armagh* which can be traced to around 807.[25] Included in the *Book of Armagh* are biographies by Muirchú (fl.

---

21. 'The Mission of Saint Patrick' in James P. Mackey, ed., *An Introduction to Celtic Christianity* (Edinburgh: T&T Clark, 1989), p, 22.

22. See Liam de Paor, *Saint Patrick's World: The Christian Culture of Ireland's Apostolic Age* (Dublin: Four Courts Press, 1996), p. 5: 'There is virtually not a single Irish artifact in a museum or a single monument in the field of which an archaeologist could say with full confidence that it was made in the fifth century.'

23. Hanson, *Life and Writings of the Historical Saint Patrick*, pp. 12-17.

24. John T. McNeill, *The Celtic Churches: A History* A.D. *200 to 1200* (Chicago, IL/London: University of Chicago Press, 1974), p. 55.

25. Hanson, *Life and Writings of the Historical Saint Patrick*, p. 15.

697) and Tírechán (fl. 690), but while their accounts provide information left out by Patrick in his own writings, they are 'tendentious and unreliable'.[26] These later biographies, which include tales of miracles and wonder workings that become increasingly fantastical the further their writing is removed from Patrick's own time, reveal that 'Patrick's life has become subject to a large amount of hagiographical embroidery and fictitious enhancement'.[27] Lastly, several references to Patrick appear in numerous later Irish records called *Annals*. Though documents like the *Annals of Insfallen* record several events from Patrick's life and even give specific dates, the fact that they are far removed temporally from the events they describe casts doubt on their accuracy.

Given this wide array of literary evidence, a biographical sketch of Patrick will be shaped undoubtedly by which sources are used. The later sources fill in portions of Patrick's life he left obscure in his own writings and have in the past been generally accepted by such scholars as the Irish historian J.B. Bury (1861–1927), who wrote the first truly authoritative biography of Patrick in 1905.[28] Without even getting into the question of the historicity of Patrick's alleged miracles as described in the later biographies, one's portrait of Patrick and his ministry will look very different if these later sources are considered reliable. In Bury's defence, it should be said that he did not have access to the last hundred years of critical scholarship about Patrick that has since called into question the wisdom of using the later literary sources to reconstruct Patrick's life. Given the unreliability of these later sources, then, this book will limit itself largely to Patrick's own two works mentioned above. Although this will curtail the material we can use, it is only this approach that can

---

26. McNeill, *Celtic Churches*, p. 66.

27. Hanson, *Life and Writings of the Historical Saint Patrick*, p. 16.

28. See J.B. Bury, *The Life of Saint Patrick and His Place in History* (London: Macmillan and Co., 1905).

guarantee a truly reliable picture of Patrick and his ministry and thought.[29]

Patrick's boyhood

The opening paragraph of Patrick's *Confession* describes his family, boyhood and captivity, and is one of the most debated portions of the entire text. Patrick introduces himself as both a 'sinner' and 'most unlearned', by which he sets a tone for the entire text that is utterly different from that of later legendary biographies that depict him as something of a 'superhuman wonder-worker'.[30]

> I am Patrick, a sinner, most unlearned (*rusticissimus*), the least of all the faithful, and utterly despised by many. My father was Calpornius, a deacon, son of Potitus, a presbyter (*presbyteri*), of the village Bannaventa Berniæ; he had a country seat nearby, and there I was taken captive. I was then about sixteen years of age. I did not know the true God. I was taken into captivity to Ireland with many thousands of people—and deservedly so, because we turned away from God, and did not keep his commandments, and did not obey our presbyters, who used to remind us of our salvation. And the Lord brought over us the wrath of his anger and scattered us among many nations, even unto the utmost part of the earth, where now my littleness is placed among strangers.[31]

Patrick's father Calpornius was a deacon and his grandfather Potitus a presbyter—Patrick was thus raised in the church. He mentions hearing the Word of God and the gospel, but admits he paid no heed to the words he heard preached. In his letter to the soldiery of the war-lord Coroticus, Patrick also notes that his

29. Hanson, *Life and Writings of the Historical Saint Patrick*, p. 18.

30. Ian Bradley, *Celtic Christianity: Making Myths and Chasing Dreams* (New York, NY: St Martin's Press, 1999), p. 12.

31. *Confession* 1, trans. Ludwig Bieler, *The Works of St Patrick, St Secundinus: Hymn on St Patrick* (Ancient Christian Writers, no.17; 1953 ed.; repr. New York/Ramsey, New Jersey: Paulist Press, n.d.), p. 21, altered.

father was an estate-owning decurion,[32] indicating that Patrick enjoyed an affluent upbringing. In E.A. Thompson's words, 'Patrick was anything but a man of the people' in his younger years.[33] A decurion was a member of the local town council. The office provided its bearer with numerous perks, but it was an onerous task, since the decurion had to pay for public entertainment, road-sweeping, and the cleaning of latrines and baths out of his own pocket. Many decurions thus either shirked their duties or were dishonest. Some scholars have suggested that Calpornius may well have become a deacon in order to escape the heavy municipal burdens that came with his decurionate, since the Christian clergy enjoyed tax-free status.[34] What Patrick was at pains to have his readers know, though, was that despite the blessing of hearing the Word of God preached in his childhood, he ignored it and as a result he 'did not know the true God'.

Patrick identifies the place where he grew up as Bannaventa Berniæ (or Bannavem Taberniæ). Regrettably, the precise name of his hometown is of little help, for not only could the name itself have been distorted through copying errors, but the only Bannaventa known to us today (a mile from the village of Norton in Northamptonshire) is nowhere near the Irish Sea and thus an unlikely place for Patrick to be captured by Irish raiders.[35] John T. McNeill summarizes the long quest to pinpoint Patrick's birthplace: 'Perhaps a dozen spots along the British coast from the Severn to the Clyde have been learnedly treated as Patrick's birthplace; but certainty has not been attained, and informed scholars have little to no expectation that it will be.'[36]

---

32. *Letter to the Soldiers of Coroticus* 10.

33. Thompson, *Who Was Saint Patrick?* p. 9.

34. Hanson, *Saint Patrick: His Origins and Career*, pp. 176-9; Freeman, *St Patrick of Ireland*, pp. 2-3.

35. Hanson, *Life and Writings of the Historical Saint Patrick*, p. 19.

36. McNeill, *Celtic Churches*, 57. See the helpful overview of possibilities in Andrew Breeze, 'St Patrick's Birthplace', *The Welsh Journal of Religious History*, 3 (2008), pp. 58-67.

But while an exact location of Bannaventa Berniæ is likely out of reach for historians, several facts about Patrick's birthplace can be known with a great degree of certainty. For example, we know that Patrick was born in Roman Britain, which despite being 'something of a backwater', was still very much Roman.[37] Furthermore, the town was likely located on or near the western coast as it would have been more susceptible to Irish raiders there than if it were further inland or on the eastern coast. Furthermore, considering Patrick's Roman upbringing, it was probably south of Hadrian's Wall.[38]

Patrick's dates

Another detail about which there is no scholarly agreement is the dating of the evangelist's life and ministry. Patrick himself gives us no date for his birth, although this has not prevented some throughout history attempting to pinpoint it to the very day and month![39] The Irish scholar Máire de Paor inclines towards a date in the second half of the fifth century for Patrick's birth and mission, placing his death around 493.[40] At the other end of the chronological spectrum, the amateur historian Mario Esposito (1887–1975), and more recently, John T. Koch, have argued for an early date of 350 or so for Patrick's birth with his death then being placed around the time of Augustine of Hippo's death in 430.[41] Basing his conclusion on evidence primarily

---

37. Hanson, *Life and Writings of the Historical Saint Patrick*, p. 5.

38. ibid., p. 19.

39. Hanson, *Saint Patrick: His Origins and Career*, p. 171.

40. De Paor, *Patrick*, p. 25. For a strong argument in favour of a later dating, see also David N. Dumville, *Saint Patrick, A.D. 493–1993* (Woodbridge, Suffolk: The Boydell Press, 1993), pp. 29-33.

41. Mario Esposito, 'The Patrician problem and a possible solution' and *idem*, 'The Problem of the Two Patricks' in his *Studies in Hiberno-Latin Literature*, ed. Michael M. Gorman (Aldershot, Hampshire/Burlington, VT: Ashgate Publishing, 2006); and John T. Koch, 'The early chronology for St Patrick (*c.* 351–*c.* 428): some new ideas and possibilities' in Jane Cartwright, ed., *Celtic Hagiography and Saints' Cults* (Cardiff: University of Wales Press, 2003), pp. 102-22.

provided by the Irish *Annals* and later lives of Patrick, J.B. Bury placed Patrick's birth around the year 389.[42] Similarly, Hanson arrives at a late fourth-century date for Patrick's birth, and he subsequently dates the end of his ministry to around 460. Hanson's conclusions, however, are reached by more reliable means than the Irish *Annals* and later biographies.

The fall of the Roman Empire

Scholars have long reflected on and debated the reasons behind the fall of the Western Roman Empire. A multitude of suggestions, ranging from the ridiculous to the extremely plausible – things like climatic change, lead poisoning of the aristocracy, excessive government bureaucracy and the demise of the urban middle class – have been made. One classical approach, that of the eighteenth-century historian Edward Gibbon (1737–1794), maintained that the fall was intimately tied to the growth of Christianity. There is no doubt that many of the most brilliant thinkers of late antiquity – men like Hilary of Poitiers, Basil of Caesarea, John Chrysostom, and Augustine of Hippo – devoted their energies to the life of the Church and not to that of the state and thereby possibly drained off valuable resources from the political sphere. But Gibbon's explanation is probably shaped as much by his bitter dislike of the Christian faith as it is by the historical evidence. Another perspective worth noting is that of Arther Ferrill, who has presented a convincing argument for a military explanation for the collapse of Roman hegemony in Western Europe. It is vital to note, however, that none of these various theories can be regarded as cogent if they do not account for why the West was submerged beneath a tidal wave of Germanic tribes while the eastern half of the Empire continued as the Byzantine Empire.

Hanson bases his view on Calporinus's status as both a decurion and deacon. As we saw, Calpornius may have become a deacon in order to evade the heavy tax burdens that came with the decurionate. By reviewing the history of legislation in

---

42. Bury, *Life of Saint Patrick*, pp. 331-4.

the Empire pertaining to this subject, Hanson concludes that the most propitious time for Calporinus to hold both offices of decurion and deacon was between 388 and 395, and hence it is likely Patrick was born during this time.[43] Additionally, Hanson links together Patrick's eschatology and the fall of the Roman Empire. In his *Confession*, Patrick speaks of living in the 'last days' of history.[44] Hanson interprets this in light of the end of the Roman Empire. Rome was sacked in 410 by Alaric, and for many, including possibly Patrick, 'the shock of this calamity was so great that many people thought that it portended the end of the world'.[45] This shock would have been reduced further into the fifth century. So again, it is likely Patrick was writing during the first half of the century nearer to the date of the sacking of Rome. We may cautiously hold, therefore, to a late fourth-century date for Patrick's birth (around 390) and an early-to-mid fifth century (roughly from 430 to 460) dating for his ministry in Ireland.[46]

Irish captivity and conversion

When Patrick was sixteen, his life of luxury was traumatically interrupted as he was 'taken into captivity to Ireland with many thousands of people'.[47] Irish raiders were common threats to the Empire, and their exploits are well documented in contemporary literature.[48] Patrick ascribes the reason for his captivity, and that of many others, to their having ignored the preaching of Christian leaders: 'we turned away from God, and did not keep

43. Hanson, *Saint Patrick: His Origins and Career*, p. 179.

44. *Confession* 34.

45. Hanson, *Saint Patrick: His Origins and Career*, p. 184. See also R.P.C. Hanson and Cécile Blanc, *Saint Patrick: Confession et Lettre à Coroticus* (Paris: Les Éditions du Cerf, 1978), pp. 18-21.

46. For other perspectives on Patrick's dates, see Thomas, *Christianity in Roman Britain*, pp. 314-46, *passim*; Thompson, *Who Was Saint Patrick?* pp. 166-75.

47. *Confession* 1.

48. De Paor, *Patrick*, p. 33; Malcolm Lambert, *Christians and Pagans: The Conversion of Britain from Alban to Bede* (New Haven/London: Yale University Press, 2010), pp. 49-51.

his commandments, and did not obey our presbyters, who used to remind us of our salvation. And the Lord brought over us the wrath of his anger and scattered us among many nations, even unto the utmost part of the earth.'[49] Here Patrick, looking back some fifty years to when the events actually took place, is drawing from the biblical prophets' critique of faithless Israel and applying the way God judged them, namely the judgment of exile, to his own day.[50]

So, at the age of sixteen, Patrick was taken captive by a band of Irish raiders and sold as a slave in Ireland. There may have been some Christians in Ireland, but they would have been few and scattered. The exact place of Patrick's captivity in Ireland is also debated among scholars, for Patrick gives us little information that would pinpoint a precise locality. At one point in the *Confession*, Patrick speaks of 'staying in the woods and on the mountains', but this is too vague to be of any real help.[51] Later in the *Confession*, when he is back in Britain, Patrick has a dream in which he hears the voices of those who were 'beside the Wood of Voclut, which is near the Western Sea' asking him to walk among them once again.[52] Hanson argues that the location of the Wood of Voclut was on the west coast of Ireland, near the modern day town of Killala, Co. Mayo, and finds confirmation for this attribution in one of Patrick's earliest biographers, Tírechán.[53] But even if the precise location of Patrick's captivity cannot be determined, the most important detail of his time as a slave in Ireland is his conversion.[54]

49. *Confession* 1.

50. See Hanson, *Life and Writings of the Historical Saint Patrick*, p. 76, in which he identifies echoes of both Isaiah and Jeremiah in this passage.

51. *Confession* 16.

52. *Confession* 23.

53. Hanson, *Life and Writings of the Historical Saint Patrick*, p. 95.

54. For a study of Patrick's experience as a slave, see Elizabeth McLuhan, '"Ministerium seruitutis meae": the metaphor and reality of slavery in Saint Patrick's *Epistola* and *Confessio*' in John Carey, Máire Herbert, and Pádraig Ó Riain, eds., *Studies in Irish hagiography: saints and scholars* (Dublin: Four Courts Press, 2001), pp. 63-71.

Having suffered the trauma of being wrenched away from home and family, Patrick turned to the living God for strength:

> And there [in Ireland] the Lord opened the understanding of my unbelieving heart that I might at last remember my sins and be converted with all my heart to the Lord my God, who had regard for my miserable state, and had mercy on my youth and ignorance, and watched over me before I knew him, and before I was able to distinguish between good and evil, and guarded me and comforted me as would a father his son.[55]

From complete indifference to religion, Patrick became convicted of his sinfulness – his living in 'death and unbelief' – and he 'earnestly sought' God.[56] The result was his whole-hearted conversion and a life-long practice of piety and self-discipline, as he noted:

> But after I came to Ireland – every day I had to tend sheep, and many times a day I prayed – the love of God and his fear came to me more and more, and my faith was strengthened. And my spirit was moved so that in a single day I would say as many as a hundred prayers, and almost as many in the night, and this even when I was staying in the woods and on the mountains; and I used to get up for prayer before daylight, through snow, through frost, through rain, and I felt no harm, and there was no sloth in me—as I now see, because the Spirit within me was then fervent.[57]

Instead of using a more general description like 'I prayed unceasingly,' Patrick, in his very concrete way of writing, emphasizes the same truth by the statement that he would utter during the day 'as many as a hundred prayers' and the same again at night. In addition to these more spontaneous prayers that issued from his heart during the day and night, Patrick also

55. *Confession* 2, trans. Bieler, 21, altered.

56. *Confession* 27 and 33, trans. Bieler, pp. 29 and 31.

57. *Confession* 16, trans. Bieler, p. 25, altered.

made a point of setting aside time before it was daylight – presumably before the chores of the day began – to pray. He obviously had to pray outdoors, hence the mention of the snow, frost and rain. And lest his readers think he was boasting of his piety in this regard, he emphasizes that it was the indwelling Holy Spirit who enabled him to persevere in this discipline of prayer. Thus Patrick, who began his captivity with little or no indication of religious piety, would eventually return to his native Britain a devout Christian.

Questions about Patrick's ministry

After spending six years in captivity, Patrick describes a dream that he had in which a voice tells him that 'soon you will go to your own country'.[58] Leaving his slave master behind, Patrick travelled two hundred miles to the ship that would carry him across the Irish Sea back to his native Britain.[59] Initially, the ship's captain refused to take Patrick on board. As Patrick was returning to the place where he had stayed the previous night, he began to pray for direction, as he was certain that God had directed him to that very spot. But before he had concluded his prayer, the captain relented and so Patrick had passage back to his homeland.[60] After describing the trip home,[61] Patrick moves rather abruptly to telling the reader that he was back in his homeland 'after a few years'.[62] Once back in Britain, Patrick now records a vision he had while dreaming. In it a man whom Patrick recognized as a certain Victoricus specifically called him to come back to Ireland.[63] Patrick relates several visions throughout his *Confession*, but unlike the visions that are common to the

---

58. *Confession* 17.
59. ibid., 18.
60. ibid.
61. ibid., 19-22.
62. ibid., 23.
63. ibid.

accounts of medieval saints, Patrick's have a kind of surrealist feel that convinces us that Patrick actually experienced them.[64] Thompson notes that this particular vision 'was one of the turning points of Patrick's life, perhaps the most critical of all'.[65] It was as a result of this vision that Patrick would eventually return to Ireland not as a slave, but as one who would spread the Christian gospel to the Irish people who had 'always worshipped idols and filthy things'.[66] It was for Patrick his personal call to the ministry of the gospel.

Patrick did not immediately go back to Ireland after this vision, but appears to have spent a number of years in preparation and theological training. Several questions have been raised and intensely debated over this detail of Patrick's mission. Did Patrick spend his time almost exclusively in Britain, or did he go to Gaul for an extended period? What kind of theological education did Patrick receive? Was Patrick sent to Ireland by the British church or the one in Gaul? Basing his conclusion largely on later Irish biographies of Patrick, Bury favours an extended stay in Gaul with Patrick making a trip to Rome during this time.[67] Similarly, Ludwig Bieler argues that it is far more probable that Patrick trained for the priesthood in Gaul than in Britain, based on the desire that Patrick expressed in *Confession* 43 to visit the brothers there.[68] Why would he express such a desire, Bieler is obviously reasoning, if he did not personally know Christians in Gaul? Bieler's sums up the order of events accordingly: Patrick was likely residing in Auxerre in Gaul when he became a candidate for the Irish mission but received opposition to his appointment from the British church, which is described in *Confession*

64. Hanson, *Life and Writings of the Historical Saint Patrick*, p. 48.

65. Thompson, *Who Was Saint Patrick?* p. 37.

66. *Confession* 41, trans. Bieler, p. 34, altered.

67. See Bury, *Life of Saint Patrick*, pp. 367-9.

68. Ludwig Bieler, 'St Patrick and the British Church' in M.W. Barley and R.P.C. Hanson, eds., *Christianity in Britain, 300–700* ([Leicester]: Leicester University Press, 1968), p. 125.

26. Despite this opposition, Patrick was later sent to Ireland as the Bishop of Ireland.[69]

Hanson argues for an alternative reconstruction, from which he concludes that Patrick's mission was sponsored by the British church. While Hanson argues that it is quite likely that Patrick did visit Gaul, his time on the continent was insignificant. Furthermore, it is unlikely he received any theological education there. In support of his view, Hanson points to Patrick's Latin. His capture by the Irish pirates robbed him of the education in rhetoric that would have been available to him because of his social stature. Referring to himself as 'most unlearned' (*rusticissimus*) or something similar on several occasions, Patrick is very conscious of his shortcomings as a writer and his inability to express himself clearly in Latin.[70] For instance, in *Confession* 9 he admits:

> I have not studied like the others, who thoroughly imbibed law and Sacred Scripture, and never had to change from the language of their childhood days, but were able to make it still more perfect. In our case, what I had to say had to be translated into a tongue foreign to me, as can be easily proved from the savour of my writing, which betrays how little instruction and training I have had in the art of words.[71]

Thus, while Patrick's contemporaries were becoming progressively skillful in their use of Latin as a literary tool, he was a slave in Ireland, having to speak the language of his captors, Old Irish. His education in Latin had been severely curtailed and when,

---

69. Bieler, 'St Patrick and the British Church,' p. 126. Sam Moorhead and David Stuttard think it possible that Patrick studied under Germanus of Auxerre (d. 437/448) while the latter was visiting in Britain in 429–430. See their *The Romans Who Shaped Britain* (London: Thames & Hudson, 2012), p. 248. This is quite feasible and might explain Patrick's desire to go to Gaul in order to renew fellowship with some Gallic Christians who might have accompanied Germanus and met Patrick at that time.

70. See *Confession* 1, 10, 11, 12, 13, 49, and 62; *Letter to the Soldiers of Coroticus* 1. See also Hanson, *Saint Patrick: His Origins and Career*, pp. 158-70; *idem*, *Life and Writings of the Historical Saint Patrick*, pp. 37-8.

71. *Confession* 9, trans. Bieler, p. 23.

much later in life, he came to write the *Confession*, he often struggled to express himself clearly.[72]

Patrick's Latin confirms his self-critiques. As Hanson notes regarding Patrick's style: 'Patrick's Latin time and time again strikes the reader as inefficient, awkward. He gropes for words; on several occasions ... he simply fails to convey what he means and we cannot be sure precisely what he is trying to say.'[73] The Latin that Patrick does know comes primarily from reading the Scriptures, not from a continental education.[74] As Christine Mohrmann points out, Patrick's Latin is 'unbookish'.[75] Had Patrick received theological training in Gaul he would have been able to read and speak Latin a lot more fluently than he can.[76] That being the case, it is more likely that Patrick was sent by the British church and not the church in Gaul (and definitely not Rome), even though it was the elders in the British church who would later bring accusations against him. Ludwig Bieler has noted that despite the fact that Patrick's preaching had to have been in Gaelic or Old Irish, his 'Latin shows no certain traces of an underlying Gaelic idiom'. Bieler believes the explanation for this to lie partly in Patrick's 'close adherence to Latin models, especially the Bible'.[77]

---

72. On Patrick's Latin, see Ludwig Bieler, 'The Place of Saint Patrick in Latin Language and Literature', *Vigiliae Christianae*, 6 (1952), pp. 65-97; Christine Mohrmann, *The Latin of Saint Patrick* (Dublin: Dublin Institute for Advanced Studies, 1961); Hanson, *Saint Patrick: His Origins and Career*, pp. 158-70; *idem* and Blanc, *Saint Patrick*, pp. 155-63.

73. Hanson, *Life and Writings of the Historical Saint Patrick*, pp. 28-9.

74. ibid., pp. 29-30. See also Mohrmann, *Latin of Saint Patrick*, pp. 8-10.

75. Mohrmann, *Latin of Saint Patrick*, p. 21. As Mohrmann explains ('The Earliest Continental Irish Latin', *Vigiliae Christianae*, 16 [1962], p. 217): 'The Latin of Patrick is clumsy, he is hampered by his bilingualism, but the structure of his language as such exhibits the characteristic traits of the living, colloquial, vulgar Latin of the fifth century. ... His Latin is not bookish, though he is continually drawing from the Bible.'

76. Hanson, *Saint Patrick: His Origins and Career*, p. 170.

77. 'St Patrick and the Irish People', *The Review of Politics*, 10 (1948), p. 294.

Christian Latin

The earliest Christians outside of Palestine primarily used Greek in their preaching and worship and writing. It was not until the end of the second century that a Christian Latin literature begins to emerge with the writings of the African theologian Tertullian. As Christianity began to express itself in Latin, it was inevitable that new words – 'Christianisms' – and new meanings for old words would appear, and thus a Christian Latin vocabulary began to develop. Words like *apostolus* (apostle), *ecclesia* (church), *episcopus* (bishop), and *confiteri* (to praise, to confess) now became a part of the language of Latin-speaking Christians. By Patrick's day, Christian Latin contained a rich vocabulary to express Christian thought. Patrick's Latin draws from this well of words, though sometimes he uses words that were not in normal Christian usage but that occurred in his Bible. In Christine Mohrmann's words: 'The influence of the Bible on his language was so great that often the biblical elements prevailed over the normal colloquial Christian vocabulary.' (*Latin of Saint Patrick*, p. 28.)

So, Patrick must then have received his theological training in Britain.[78] This would have taken place in the late 410s and 420s. In the course of this preparation, he became thoroughly familiar with the Latin Bible, so much so that Christine Mohrmann has rightly described Patrick as 'a man *unius libri*' ('a man of one book').[79] Like other Fathers of the ancient church, Patrick also definitely came to know large tracts of the Latin Bible by heart. It was not only when he was formally citing Scripture that the Latin Bible appears, but even when Patrick was writing his own words the Scriptures are ever in view, shaping thought and vocabulary.[80]

---

78. See also Lambert, *Christians and Pagans*, pp. 137-8.

79. Mohrmann, *Latin of Saint Patrick*, p. 8. On Patrick's devotion to the Scriptures, see below, Chapter 4.

80. Mohrmann, *Latin of Saint Patrick*, p. 43: in Patrick's writings, 'there is a sort of omnipresence of Holy Scripture'.

Patrick's Irish mission

Finally, in this first chapter we must mention Patrick's accomplishments during his ministry as Bishop of Ireland.[81] Following the arguments of Hanson, Patrick's ministry in Ireland falls roughly between 430 and 460. In his *Confession*, Patrick tells us on more than one occasion of the many converts, sometimes numbering in the thousands, who were brought to a living faith in Christ throughout his ministry.[82] These converts range from the lowest of Irish society to the highest, from slaves and widows to the sons and daughters of Irish kings.[83] Unlike the otherworldly miracle worker depicted by later biographies of Patrick, the two authentic writings from Patrick reveal a typical fifth-century bishop who was involved in preaching, baptizing, celebrating the Lord's Supper, confirming new converts, and ordaining ministers.[84] While we may lament the fact that many specific details of Patrick's life remain obscure, Hanson is surely correct in saying that we can nevertheless know him intimately, as we shall see in the chapters that follow.[85] And though he lived on the fringes of a dying empire more than 1,500 years ago, today Patrick's name is probably 'more widely known throughout the world than the names of Jerome and Augustine and even Constantine the Great'.[86]

---

81. For a more complete study of Patrick's mission, see Chapter 3.

82. See *Confession* 14, 38, 41, 50.

83. *Confession* 42.

84. Hanson and Blanc, *Saint Patrick*, p. 39.

85. Hanson, *Life and Writings of the Historical Saint Patrick*, p. 54.

86. Thompson, *Who Was Saint Patrick?* p. 15.

2

'ONE GOD IN THE TRINITY OF THE HOLY NAME':
The Divine Foundation of Patrick's Theology

Patrick is 'a man *unius libri*' — 'a man of one book'.[1] This description of Patrick by Christine Mohrmann highlights the important
fact that, apart from one extended citation, Patrick never clearly
references any other text than his Latin Bible.[2] That citation occurs very near the beginning of his *Confession* and is a credal statement that clearly does not come from his hand.[3] It runs as follows:

> There is no other God, nor ever was in times past, nor will be
> hereafter, than God the Father unbegotten, without beginning,
> from whom is all beginning, who holds sway over all things

1. Christine Mohrmann, *The Latin of Saint Patrick* (Dublin: Dublin Institute for Advanced Studies, 1961), p, 8.

2. See, for example, the examination of the claim that Patrick knew Augustine's *Con-
fessions* by J. O'Meara, 'Patrick's *Confessio* and Augustine's *Confessiones*' in his and
Bernd Naumann, eds., *Latin Script and Letters* A.D. *400–900. Festschrift presented to
Ludwig Bieler on the occasion of his 70th birthday* (Leiden: E.J. Brill, 1976), pp. 44-53.
See also the discussion of works that Patrick may have known by Mohrmann, *Latin
of Saint Patrick*, pp. 7-8; R.P.C. Hanson, *The Life and Writings of the Historical Saint
Patrick* (New York, NY: Seabury Press, 1983), pp. 42-3.

3. Hanson, *Life and Writings of the Historical Saint Patrick*, pp. 79, 81. According to
D.R. Bradley, 'The Doctrinal Formula of Patrick', *Journal of Theological Studies*, n.s.,
33 (1982), pp. 124-33, the Latin of the first half of this creed has the 'balance and
cadences of what passed for polished style in late antiquity' (p. 125) and is clearly
not of Patrick's own composition. And although the second half of the creed is
filled with biblical quotation or allusion, it too has regular cadences.

(*omnia tenentem*),[4] as we declare; and his Son Jesus Christ, whom
we affirm most assuredly to have always been with the Father
before the origin of the world, spiritually and ineffably begotten
by the Father before all beginning, and by him all things visible
and invisible were made; he was made man, and when death had
been overcome, he was received into heaven beside the Father;
'and he has given him all power over every name in heaven and
on earth and under the earth, and every tongue will confess to
him that Jesus Christ is Lord and God',[5] in whom we believe and
to whose imminent coming we look forward, 'the judge of the
living and of the dead',[6] 'who will render to every man according
to his deeds'[7]; and 'he has poured forth upon us abundantly the
Holy Spirit',[8] 'the gift' and 'pledge'[9] of immortality, who makes
those who believe and obey 'sons of God and co-heirs with
Christ'[10]: it is him that we confess (*confitemur*) and adore, one
God in the Trinity of the holy name.[11]

R.P.C. Hanson has drawn attention to the fact that there are
some definite parallels between this creed and a doctrinal formula
drawn up by Victorinus of Pettau (Poetoevium), a bishop from the
Roman province of Pannonia, which stretched from the Danube
into the Balkans, and who died as a martyr around A.D. 304 in the
persecution unleashed by the Roman emperor Diocletian. While
Patrick's confession is probably the rule of faith of the church in
which he was raised, namely, the church in Britain, the similarities

---

4. Ludwig Bieler argues that *omnia tenentem* should be translated as 'Lord of the universe'. See his *Libri Epistolarum Sancti Patricii Episcopi. Part II: Commentary* (Dublin: Stationery Office, 1952), pp. 98-9.

5. Philippians 2:9-11

6. Acts 10:42

7. Romans 2:6

8. Titus 3:5. For the reading 'us,' see R.P.C. Hanson, 'The Rule of Faith of Victorinus and of Patrick' in J.J. O'Meara and B. Naumann, eds., *Latin Script and Letters A.D.400–900. Festschrift presented to Ludwig Bieler* (Leiden: E.J. Brill, 1976), pp. 35-6.

9. cf. Acts 2:38; Ephesians 1:14

10. Romans 8:16-17

11. *Confession* 4, trans. Michael A.G. Haykin.

with Victorinus's creed would seem to indicate that this rule of faith ultimately derives from that of Victorinus.[12] But, as Hanson readily admits, Victorinus's creed has been reshaped to address theological realities at the close of the fourth century, namely, the issues raised by the Arian controversy. What is noticeably absent are any references to fifth-century Christological issues that centred on issues relating to the way that the divinity and humanity were one person in Jesus of Nazareth.[13]

The creed needs to be read in its surrounding context. In the section immediately preceding this confession, Patrick has stressed that he must 'exalt and confess (*confiteri*) [God's] wondrous works before every nation',[14] works that include his own conversion. And in the passage that follows, Tobit 12:7, part of the Apocrypha, is cited to make a similar point: 'It is honourable to reveal and confess (*confiteri*) the works of God.'[15] The credal statement is thus bookended by the 'heart's desire' of Patrick to be a confessor

12. Hanson, 'Rule of Faith of Victorinus and of Patrick' in O'Meara and Naumann, eds., *Latin Script and Letters*, pp. 25-36; *idem* and Cécile Blanc, *Saint Patrick: Confession et Lettre à Coroticus* (Sources chrétiennes, no. 249; Paris: Les Éditions du Cerf, 1978), pp. 75-7, nn. 2-4; R.P.C. Hanson, 'Witness from St Patrick to the Creed of 381', *Analecta Bollandiana*, 101 (1983), pp. 297-9.

On the confession and its background, see also John Ernest Leonard Oulton, *The Credal Statements of St Patrick as Contained in the Fourth Chapter of his Confession. A Study of Their Sources* (Dublin: Hodges, Figgis & Co./London: Oxford University Press, 1940); Ludwig Bieler, 'The "Creeds" of St Victorinus and St Patrick', *Theological Studies*, 9 (1949), pp. 121-4.

On Victorinus, see William Smith and Henry Wace, eds., *A Dictionary of Christian Biography* (London: John Murray, 1887), 4:1128-1129 and C. Curti, 'Victorinus of Petovium' in Angelo Di Berardino, *Encyclopedia of the Early Church*, trans. Adrian Walford (New York, NY: Oxford University Press, 1992), 2:867. Jonathan J. Armstrong has recently argued that Victorinus is the author of the famous list of the New Testament canon, the Muratorian Fragment: 'Victorinus of Pettau as the Author of the Canon Muratori', *Vigiliae Christianae*, 62 (2008), pp. 1-34.

13. Hanson, 'Witness from St Patrick to the Creed of 381', p. 297; *idem*, 'Rule of Faith of Victorinus and of Patrick' in O'Meara and Naumann, eds., *Latin Script and Letters*, p. 32.

14. *Confession* 3, trans. Ludwig Bieler, *The Works of St Patrick, St Secundinus: Hymn on St Patrick* (Ancient Christian Writers, no. 17; 1953 ed.; repr. New York/Ramsey, New Jersey: Paulist Press, n.d.), p. 22, altered.

15. *Confession* 5, trans. Bieler, p. 22.

of God's great works[16] – and these works involve not simply his own conversion, but supremely God's work of salvation in Christ.

Moreover, by placing these three sections at the very beginning of his narrative, Patrick seems to have intended that these sections help explain what he intended by the Latin title of his work: *Confessio*. This Latin word can bear three meanings: acknowledgment of sin, a credal declaration of one's core beliefs, and a declaration of praise. Undoubtedly, there are elements of all three of these meanings in Patrick's *Confession*. But the contextual placement of these three sections including the creed would seem to indicate that the book is especially an acknowledgment of deep thanks on Patrick's part for God's amazing grace and work – in his life, among the Irish, and, most of all, in Christ. In other words, the reason for Patrick's inclusion of the creed is not because his orthodoxy has been questioned, as some commentators have suggested. Rather, it has to do with Patrick's desire to praise his Triune Lord.[17]

The relationship of the Father and the Son

The creed begins with a confession of monotheism: there is only one true God. This dogmatic assertion was, of course, utterly needed in the polytheistic environment of Celtic Ireland. The one true God is also a Triune being: the Father and his Son, the Lord Jesus Christ, and the Holy Spirit. Here Patrick broaches one of the most profound truths of the Christian faith. Along with such Christian doctrines as the incarnation and the atoning work of Christ, the Trinity is a revealed truth that surpasses the ability of human reason to fully comprehend it, but nevertheless must be articulated as far as we are able by rational discourse.

The Father is confessed to be 'unbegotten [and] without beginning'. The term 'unbegotten' in the language of early Church Fathers like Athanasius and Basil of Caesarea (c. 329–

16. *Confession* 6.

17. Thomas O'Loughlin, *Discovering Saint Patrick* (London: Darton, Longman and Todd, 2005), pp. 141-2, n. 1; Oulton, *Credal Statements of St Patrick*, p. 10. For a somewhat different perspective, see Mohrmann, *Latin of Saint Patrick*, pp. 4-7.

379) emphasizes the fact that the Father is without origin, has the source of his being within himself, and is the One who has made all things.[18] Or, as Patrick's creed puts it: he is 'without beginning'. The Father also 'holds sway over all things'. God's sovereignty was not only an article of doctrinal confession for Patrick, but also an important existential reality. To an outsider in Ireland like Patrick, one without the network of protection that came from being a part of Irish society, the conviction of God's dominion over all things would have been deeply meaningful.[19] A number of times Patrick clearly saw God's sovereignty in his life. For instance, after Patrick had escaped from captivity and was on his way back to Britain, the sailors with whom he was travelling ran out of food, and their captain challenged Patrick: 'Tell me, Christian: you say that your God is great and all-powerful (*omnipotens*); why, then, do you not pray for us? As you can see, we are suffering from hunger; it is unlikely indeed that we shall ever see a human being again.' Patrick responded by urging them to wholeheartedly trust in the Lord and to know that nothing is impossible for him. In their hunger he saw an opportunity to urge them to exercise saving faith. And within a very short period of time – Patrick does not specify how long – a herd of pigs appeared that gave them food enough for not only themselves but also their dogs.[20] Much later, when Patrick was faced on a daily basis with the possibility of 'murder, fraud, or captivity' during his ministry in Ireland, his response was to affirm his trust in a sovereign God: 'I fear none of these things because ... I have cast myself into the hands of God Almighty, who rules everywhere.'[21]

---

18. Athanasius, *On the Decrees of Council of Nicaea* 30–31; Kevin Giles, *The Eternal Generation of the Son: Maintaining Orthodoxy in Trinitarian Theology* (Downers Grove, IL: InterVarsity Press, 2012), pp. 125-34.

19. Dana L. Robert, 'Conversion and Christian Community: The Missionary from St Patrick to Bernard Mizeki' in his *Christian Mission: How Christianity Became A World Religion* (Malden, MA/Oxford/Chichester, West Sussex: Wiley-Blackwell, 2009), pp. 148-9.

20. *Confession* 19.

21. *Confession* 55, trans. Bieler, p. 38.

Typical of creeds of the ancient church, the second major section deals with the Lord Jesus. The relationship of the Lord Jesus to God the Father is first of all treated. He is the Son of the Father. As the early Christian theologian Tertullian had argued: 'The Father must necessarily have a Son in order to be a Father, and the Son a Father to be Son.'[22] There can never have been a time when the Father was without his Son and not therefore the Father. The Lord Jesus must, therefore, be confessed to have 'always been with the Father'. In other words, the Lord Jesus has always existed as a distinct divine person beside the Father. Therefore, contrary to those in the fourth century who claimed that the Son was inferior to the Father and a creature – known as the Arians after Arius (died c. 336), who first propagated this heretical view – the Son cannot be considered a creature.

The teaching of Arius

Arius, an elder of the church at Alexandria in Egypt, was probably born in Libya somewhere between 260 and 280. Of his career before 318 little certain is known. It seems he studied in Antioch and was ordained as an elder in either 312 or 313. Around 318 or 319, Arius began to propagate views which caused no small stir in the Egyptian and Libyan Christian community. Arius maintained that only the Father was truly God. As he wrote in a letter to Alexander (d. 328), the Bishop of Alexandria, God the Father alone, 'the cause of all, is without beginning'. The Son was created by the Father as 'an immutable and unchangeable perfect creature', and thus is 'not everlasting or co-everlasting with the Father'. In Arius' words: 'the Son has a beginning, but God is without beginning'. Thus, for Arius and his followers, though the Son can be called God, he is 'not God as God is God'. As for the Holy Spirit, by Arius's reckoning, he was even less divine than the Son, for he was the first of the creatures made by the Son. These teachings helped spark what we name the Arian controversy, which led to the church not only issuing what we call the Nicene Creed, but also led to some of the richest biblical reflection on this key doctrine. Patrick's faith is rooted in this reflection.

---

22. Tertullian, *Against Praxeas*, 10.

Furthermore, the Son, the Lord Jesus, was 'spiritually and ineffably begotten by the Father'. Building upon the identification of the first two persons of the Godhead as Father and Son, early Christian theologians argued that the identifying mark of the Father's personhood can be described as 'unbegotten,' while that of the second person of the Godhead, the Son, must be described as 'begotten'. By using such descriptions, Christian authors were seeking to safeguard the indelible differentiation of the Son from the Father and so avoid what is called modalism, another heresy that especially dogged the church of the early Christian era. Modalism collapses the persons of the Father and the Son into one and the same person, thereby endangering the divine work of redemption. For instance, if the Father and the Son are the same person, then who was propitiated by the Son's death on the cross (see 1 John 2:2; Hebrews 9:14)?[23]

The fatherhood of the Father and the sonship of the Son, of course, differ from the human relation of father and son. To understand the generation of the divine Son from God the Father in human terms would be to sully the truth of Scripture.[24] Hence, the Son's generation from the Father is described as having taken place 'spiritually and ineffably (*inenarrabiliter*).' And because the Son has always been with the Father, this generation from the Father must be eternal, and, as such, bears witness to the fact that the Father and the Son share one being, since there is only one true and living God. And as God, the Son was also vitally involved in the creation of 'all things visible and invisible'.

The Lord Jesus Christ

Now, wonder of wonders, the Son of God became man for the salvation of sinners like Patrick. It is curious that this creed

---

23. For a brief discussion of modalism, see Michael A.G. Haykin, 'And did the Father die? Discerning the error of Modalism' in his *Defence of the Truth: Contending for the truth yesterday and today* (Darlington, England/Webster, NY: Evangelical Press, 2004), pp. 125-9.

24. Giles, *Eternal Generation of the Son*, p. 128.

makes no explicit mention of Christ's crucifixion,[25] though in his *Letter to the Soldiers of Coroticus* Patrick does refer to some newly baptized believers taken captive by Coroticus as those 'for whom he [i.e. Christ] died and was crucified'.[26] The creed does refer to the victory of Christ's resurrection over death and his ascension to heaven, where the Father has made him Lord over all – the latter affirmed by means of the citation of Philippians 2:9-11. Elsewhere in the *Confession*, Patrick refers to Christ as 'our Redeemer',[27] 'my Lord',[28] and 'my God',[29] and to himself as 'a slave in Christ'.[30] The depth of Patrick's devotion to Christ is well seen in a statement that he makes after thanking God for keeping him faithful during a time of temptation: 'today I can confidently offer him my soul as a living sacrifice – to Christ my Lord who saved me out of all my troubles'.[31]

The section on Christ concludes with a statement about him as the coming Judge, 'to whose imminent coming we look forward, "the judge of the living and of the dead, who will render to every man according to his deeds"'. As John Carey has noted, little has been written about Patrick's eschatological beliefs, that is, his view of the end times.[32] And yet, Patrick's conviction that

---

25. Oulton, *Credal Statements of St Patrick*, p. 10.

26. *Letter to the Soldiers of Coroticus* 7.

27. *Confession* 59.

28. *Confession* 20, 30, 34, 44. See also *Confession* 43 and 55, where Christ is described as 'the Lord'. It is not always clear that Patrick has Christ in mind when he uses the term 'Lord'.

29. *Letter to the Soldiers of Coroticus* 5.

30. *Letter to the Soldiers of Coroticus* 10.

31. *Confession* 34, trans. Bieler, p. 31. See also N.J.D. White, *The Teaching of Saint Patrick* (St Patrick's Commemoration Booklets, no. 2; Dublin: Association for Promotion of Christian Knowledge, 1932), p. 3: 'One of the most noticeable elements in the personal life of St Patrick, as reflected in his writings, was the intensity of his devotion to our Lord Jesus Christ.' As White notes, it is not without significance that the Virgin Mary, a prominent figure of devotion in Irish Roman Catholicism, is never once mentioned by Patrick (*Teaching of Saint Patrick*, p. 4).

32. 'Saint Patrick, the Druids, and the End of the World', *History of Religions*, 36 (1996), p. 49.

history would end very soon is essential to his understanding of his mission. While much of Patrick's creed goes back to that of Victorinus of Pettau, this emphasis on the imminence of the second coming does not.[33] Patrick was assured that Christ was coming back to earth soon since his mission to Ireland had been to people living at the farthest extremity of the world:

> Whatever happens to me, be it good or evil, I ought always to accept it and give thanks to God, who showed me that I can trust him always without any doubts, and who must have heard my prayer so that I, however ignorant (*inscius*) I was, in the last days dared to undertake such a holy and wonderful work—thus imitating somehow those who, as the Lord once foretold, would preach his Gospel for a testimony to all nations before the end of the world. So we have seen it, and so it has been fulfilled: indeed, we are witnesses that the Gospel has been preached unto those parts beyond which there lives nobody.[34]

Patrick knew the import of the prophetic word of Matthew 24:14 that, before the end of time, the gospel would be preached to the ends of the earth. And since, as he believed, he had been involved in the evangelization of those who inhabited the edge of the world, then Christ must be returning soon.[35]

The text from the Gospel of Matthew is cited again in a series of biblical texts on mission that Patrick quotes in *Confession* 40.[36] Among the other passages that are cited is Jeremiah 16:16, where God envisages how he will return the Israelites from their exile in Babylon to the land of Israel: God will send for 'many fishermen' who will catch his people like a fisher catches fish, and he will 'send for many hunters', who will hunt for God's people in the mountains and hills, and retrieve them from 'the crevices of the rocks'. Patrick cites this Jeremiah text also in his *Letter to the*

---

33. 'Saint Patrick, the Druids, and the End of the World', *History of Religions*, 36 (1996), p. 49.

34. *Confession* 34, trans. Bieler, 31, altered.

35. Carey, 'Saint Patrick, the Druids, and the End of the World', pp. 49-50.

36. For this catena, see below in Chapter 3.

Soldiers of Coroticus, where he explicitly includes himself as 'one of his [that is, God's] hunters or fishers whom God once foretold would come in the last days'.[37] As John Carey notes, these texts constitute 'unambiguous evidence that eschatology was of primary importance' to Patrick, since he regarded his Irish mission as a key part of the spread of the gospel to the very ends of the earth, which, when it was complete, would usher in the return of Christ.[38]

Patrick is also deeply interested in the theme of Christ as judge. For instance, he insists that he is striving to tell the truth about his life in the *Confession* since he knows that 'absolutely every one of us shall give an account, even of our smallest sins before the judgment seat of Christ'.[39] His *Letter to the Soldiers of Coroticus* is, of course, dominated by the theme of judgment. Like many other aspects about Patrick's life and ministry, the identity of Coroticus is the subject of much scholarly debate.[40] What is clear from Patrick's letter is that Coroticus was a brutal war-lord, whose soldiers executed a raid that led to the enslavement of some of Patrick's newly-baptized converts – subsequently sold as slaves to the Scots and those whom Patrick calls 'the abominable, wicked, and apostate Picts'[41] – while others ended up being 'butchered and slaughtered with the sword'.[42] In response, Patrick does not mince his words: Coroticus and his band of criminals are 'rebels against Christ' and will end up 'enslaved in the eternal punishment of Gehenna' with the devil if they do not repent.[43] Coursing

---

37. *Letter to the Soldiers of Coroticus* 11, trans. Bieler, 44, altered.

38. Carey, 'Saint Patrick, the Druids, and the End of the World', pp. 50-1.

39. *Confession* 8, trans. Bieler, 23, altered. Patrick deems truth-telling to be a vital aspect of the Christian life: see *Confession* 7-8, 31, 44, 48, 54, 61.

40. See, for example, E.A. Thompson, 'St Patrick and Coroticus', *Journal of Theological Studies*, n.s., 31 (1980), 12-27; David N. Dumville, *Saint Patrick, A.D. 493-1993* (Woodbridge, Suffolk: Boydell Press, 1993), 107-27.

41. *Letter to the Soldiers of Coroticus* 15, trans. Bieler, p. 41.

42. *Letter to the Soldiers of Coroticus* 3, trans. Bieler, p. 41.

43. ibid., p. 46; *Letter to the Soldiers of Coroticus* 4, trans. Bieler, p. 42. It is noteworthy that even at this eleventh hour for Coroticus and those under his command, Patrick held out the possibility of conversion (*Letter to the Soldiers of Coroticus* 21).

through this letter is a keen sense that there is coming a day of reckoning when all will be made right and evildoers judged. It bears noting, though, that Patrick knows himself to be a sinner also deeply in need of forgiveness. As he states:

> I do not trust myself as long as I am in this body of death, for strong is he who daily strives to turn me away from the faith and the purity of true religion to which I have devoted myself to Christ my Lord to the end of my life. But the hostile flesh is ever dragging me towards death, that is, towards the forbidden satisfaction of one's desires; and I know that in part I have not led a perfect life ... but ... thanks to the grace of God, I have kept the faith.[44]

The Holy Spirit

A small catena of biblical citations and allusions serves to express Patrick's convictions regarding the Holy Spirit. The Spirit has been poured out upon the people of God (Titus 3:5). He is the 'gift' (Acts 2:38) and 'pledge' (Eph. 1:14) of immortality. Without the gift of the Spirit, men and women are in a state of spiritual death. And our works do not merit the gift of the Spirit, for, like Patrick, all are sinners. God's bestowal of his Spirit upon believers is thus an act of sheer grace.

Patrick's strong emphasis upon the grace of God at various points in his narrative is probably due to the Pelagian controversy, which spanned the fifth century and was not resolved until the Council of Orange (529).[45] Pelagius, a British monk, argued that the human will was sufficiently free to obey God and his commands without the aid of divine grace and therefore potentially able to

---

44. *Confession* 44, trans. Bieler, p. 35, altered.

45. Mohrmann, *Latin of Saint Patrick*, p. 25; L. Bieler, 'Patrick, St', *New Catholic Encyclopedia* (Washington, DC: Catholic University of America, 1967), 10:1100; Clare Stancliffe, 'Patrick (*fl.* 5th cent.)', *Oxford Dictionary of National Biography*, Oxford University Press, 2004 (http://www.oxforddnb.com.libaccess.lib.mcmaster.ca/view/article/21562, accessed October 23, 2013): 'Patrick's strong theology of grace ... does suggest that his period of training fell at the time of the Pelagian controversy in Britain.'

lead a sinless life.[46] In the words of J.N.L. Myres, Pelagianism encouraged an 'attitude of self-reliance' and emphasized 'the saving quality of a virtuous life'.[47] His main theological opponent was Augustine of Hippo, whose writings against Pelagius and his allies celebrated the sovereignty of God's grace in the salvation of sinners.[48] There is good evidence that Pelagianism was popular in certain circles in Britain — Germanus of Auxerre (died c. 437/448), for example, was sent to Britain by Celestine, Bishop of Rome, to stem the tide of Pelagianism in 429.[49] While Patrick does not explicitly refer to this controversy, his consciousness of being an object of divine grace would have made him strongly supportive of the anti-Pelagianism expressed by Augustine.

Germanus of Auxerre

Our knowledge of the life of Germanus is largely based on a biographical work by Constantius of Lyons, written some twenty to thirty years after the bishop's death. Despite numerous hagiographical elements, this biography is a key source for knowledge about fifth-century Britain after the close of Roman rule. In it, Constantius records Germanus's trip to Britain around 429 to combat Pelagianism. He is depicted as preaching not only in churches, but 'at crossroads, in the fields, and in the lanes' and succeeds in winning many back from the heresy. A decisive debate with a leading Pelagian named Agricola took place at Verulamium (present-day St Albans). Germanus also enabled a Romano-British army to win a military victory over a marauding band of Picts and Saxons. On Easter Sunday, Germanus, who had had military

---

46.   Gerald Bonner, 'Pelagianism' in Trevor A. Hart et al., eds., The Dictionary of Historical Theology (Grand Rapids, MI: William B. Eerdmans Publ. Co., 2000), pp. 422-4.

47.   'Pelagius and the End of Roman Rule in Britain', The Journal of Roman Studies, 50 (1960), pp. 28-9.

48.   See the overview of the Pelagian Controversy by Eugene TeSelle, 'Pelagius, Pelagianism' in Allan D. Fitzgerald et al., eds., Augustine through the Ages: An Encyclopedia (Grand Rapids, MI/Cambridge, UK: William B. Eerdmans Publ. Co., 1999), pp. 633-40.

49.   R.P.C. Hanson, Saint Patrick: His Origins and Career (Oxford: Clarendon Press, 1968), pp. 35-50.

experience, positions the Romano-British soldiers in a narrow defile with mountains on either side. When the Picts and Saxons arrive in the glen, Germanus instructs the soldiers to yell in unison the word 'Alleluia' as a battle cry. As the sound of this yell echoes and re-echoes in the mountains, the enemy are thrown into terror and confusion, and flee without striking a blow.

In popular media, Italian actor Ivano Marescotti has portrayed Germanus as cruel and arrogant (not true to Constantius' account) in the 2004 movie *King Arthur*, where the legendary Arthur (played by Clive Owen) is also depicted as being a disciple of Pelagius!

When Patrick confessed that it had been 'the Lord [who] opened the sense of my unbelief' and led him to faith in Christ during his captivity, this was nothing less than 'great grace (*tantam gratiam*)' and ultimately the work of the Holy Spirit.[50] His subsequent ministry in Ireland that led to the conversion and baptism of thousands is described similarly: it was an act of 'great grace,' of which Patrick was not worthy.[51] And the fact that Patrick stayed true to the Faith was, in the final analysis, due to God's grace.[52]

Moreover, it is the Spirit's grace that makes sinners 'sons of God and co-heirs with Christ'. Close to the end of the *Confession* Patrick reiterates this phrase when he declares his confidence in the resurrection: 'without doubt we shall rise ... in the glory of Christ Jesus our Redeemer, as sons of the living God and co-heirs with Christ, to be made conformable to his image'.[53] The Spirit's work in making Christians the children of God the Father and 'co-heirs with Christ' obviously has significance for this world, for a loving God watches over those who are his children in this life.[54] But this work of the Spirit is also rich with implications

---

50. *Confession* 2–3, trans. Bieler, p. 21. See also *Confession* 36: the ability 'to know God and to love him' is a divine gift. For the pneumatological interpretation of Patrick's conversion, see Noel Dermot O'Donoghue, *Aristocracy of Soul: Patrick of Ireland* (Wilmington, DE: Michael Glazier, 1987), pp. 43-5.

51. *Confession* 14–15, 38, 46, 51; *Letter to the Soldiers of Coroticus* 5.

52. *Confession* 44.

53. *Confession* 59, trans. Bieler, p. 39, altered.

54. See, for example, *Confession* 2.

for the world to come. In the confession cited above, Patrick describes the Spirit as the 'pledge of immortality', an allusion to Ephesians 1:14.[55] The believer's experience of the Spirit in this world is a foretaste of a much richer experience in the world to come. As Patrick affirms in *Confession* 59, Christians, as those indwelt by the Holy Spirit and as sons of God and co-heirs with Christ, will be raised from the dead 'in the glory of Christ', their redeemer, and their humanity remade like Christ's glorified humanity.[56] Christians will thus be preserved from eternal destruction, for they are joined to 'Christ, [who] lives for ever'.[57]

Confessing and adoring the Trinity

When the Arian controversy was finally resolved theologically at the Council of Constantinople in 381, a credal statement was issued. It is technically called the Niceno-Constantinopolitan Creed, but is popularly known as the Nicene Creed, for it was basically a reworking of the Nicene Creed issued at the Council of Nicaea in 325, right at the very beginning of the Arian crisis. In the article dealing with the Holy Spirit that was issued in 381, it is stated, among other things, that the Holy Spirit 'is worshipped and glorified with the Father and the Son'. This is an unequivocal declaration of the Spirit's deity: if he is worshipped along with the Father and the Son, and given divine honours along with them, then he must be as fully God as they are. This all-important af-firmation in the Nicene Creed seems to be reflected in Patrick's confession: the Spirit,[58] along with the Father and the Son, is to be confessed as God and adored. In the final reference to the Trinity in the *Confession*, Patrick states that the three persons of the God-head — the Father, Christ, and the Holy Spirit—reigned before this

---

55. Hanson, 'Rule of Faith of Victorinus and of Patrick' in O'Meara and Naumann, eds., *Latin Script and Letters*, pp. 29-30.

56. For more on the Spirit's work, see below, Chapter 4.

57. *Confession* 59, trans. Bieler, p. 40, altered.

58. Hanson, 'Witness from St Patrick to the Creed of 381,' p. 299.

world existed, just as they reign even now, and will do so forever and ever.[59] Hence, for Christians who worship the true God, they adore 'one God in the Trinity of the holy name'.

The Trinity is explicitly mentioned in two other passages in Patrick's two works: at the close of Patrick's epistle to Coroticus's men, and in *Confession* 14, where faith in the Trinity is cited as a reason for Patrick's Irish mission. In the former, Patrick oddly concludes: 'Peace be to the Father, and to the Son, and to the Holy Spirit.'[60] Ludwig Bieler suggests that since Patrick can hardly conclude the letter with a wish of peace for the soldiers of the war-lord, the evangelist 'concludes with a wish that peace may be restored with the Holy Trinity, in other words, that the guilty should make their peace with God.'[61] In this case, possibly the benediction should be translated thus: 'May there be peace with the Father and the Son and the Holy Spirit.' There is no doubt that Patrick wanted to see repentance from Coroticus and his men. Just before this mention of the Trinity he prayed for them: 'May God inspire them ... to recover their senses ..., repenting, however late, their heinous deeds ... and to set free the baptized women whom they took captive.'[62] Or it could be simply the case that there is a genuine grammatical confusion in Patrick's expression.[63]

The Breastplate of Patrick

The Old Irish prayer, *The Breastplate of Patrick*, though most likely written in the century following Patrick's death, is an excellent example of the way in which Patrick's Trinitarian faith was transmitted in the Celtic church. In its opening and closing refrain, it declares:

59. *Confession* 60.

60. *Letters to the Soldiers of Coroticus* 21, trans. Bieler, p. 47, altered.

61. Bieler, *Works of St Patrick*, p. 94, n. 58.

62. *Letters to the Soldiers of Coroticus* 21, trans. Bieler, p. 47, altered.

63. Richard P.C. Hanson and Cécile Blanc, *Saint Patrick: Confession et Lettre à Coroticus* (Sources Chrétiennes, no.249; Paris: Les Éditions du Cerf, 1978), p. 153, n. 6.

> For my shield this day I call:
> A mighty power:
> The Holy Trinity!
> Affirming threeness,
> Confessing oneness ... (Trans. N.D. O'Donoghue)

Confession 14, on the other hand, is crystal clear in the way it grounds mission in the Triunity of God. As Patrick states:

> With respect to the rule of faith in the Trinity (*in mensura ... fidei Trinitatis*), it is my duty, *without concern for dangers, to make known the gift of God and his eternal consolation, to spread everywhere the name of God without fear and with confidence, so that even after my death I may leave a bequest (exagaellias) to my brothers and sons I have baptized in the Lord—so many thousands of people.*[64]

At the heart of the Gospel that Patrick preached in Ireland was the Trinity: the Father who planned the work of salvation, the Son who became man and died for the salvation of sinners, and the Spirit who brings home the Father's plan and Son's work to sinful human beings and makes them, as the confession has stated, 'sons of God and co-heirs with Christ'. Ludwig Bieler was right to see in this Trinitarian declaration 'a key-note, a motto of the whole work': Patrick 'wants us to see the experiences of his life and the fulfillment of his mission in the light of his belief in the Holy Trinity.'[65] And despite the dangers that attended itinerant evangelism in fifth-century Ireland, Patrick knew it to be his duty to declare this gospel wherever he could. To that mission we now turn.

---

64. *Confession* 14, trans. Michael A.G. Haykin. For the translation of 'bequest,' see Ludwig Bieler, 'Exagellia', *The American Journal of Philology*, 69 (1948), pp. 309-12.

65. *Libri Epistolarum Sancti Patricii Episcopi. Part II: Commentary* (Dublin: Stationery Office, 1952), p. 97.

3

'I AM BOUND BY THE SPIRIT':
Patrick and his Irish Mission

When William Carey (1761–1834), Joshua Marshman (1768–1837) and William Ward (1769–1823) summarized the principles upon which they would base their mission at Serampore in India, they drew a comparison between what they were assured would happen in India and what God had done in the British Isles nearly fifteen hundred years earlier.

> He who raised the sottish and brutalised Britons to sit in heavenly places in Christ Jesus, can raise these slaves of superstition, purify their hearts by faith, and make them worshippers of the one God in spirit and in truth. The promises are fully sufficient to remove our doubts, and to make us anticipate that not very distant period when He will famish all the gods of India, and cause these very idolaters to cast their idols to the moles and to the bats, and renounce for ever the work of their own hands.[1]

Despite the immense task facing them in India, they had confidence in the God who had brought their distant ancestors, also 'slaves of superstition', to a genuine faith in Christ. Thirteen years earlier, in 1792, Carey had made a number of references to this evangelization of the British Isles in his epoch-making work, *An Enquiry into the Obligations of Christians, to Use Means for the Conversion of the Heathens.*

---

1. *The Serampore Form of Agreement* I in 'The Serampore Form of Agreement', *The Baptist Quarterly*, 12 (1946–1948), p. 130.

He did so by distinguishing between those missions that sought to expand the dominion of 'popery', usually 'by force of arms', and those that genuinely extended the kingdom of Christ.

Patrick in the nineteeth century

William Carey was not alone in his citing of Patrick as a missionary hero to be emulated. In *The Baptist Magazine*, an English journal that began publication in the first decade of the nineteenth century, 'the heroic labours of Patrick' were recalled in a two-part article in 1879. It was these labours, the anonymous article argued, that led to Ireland being 'rescued from her old Druidical superstitions, and enlightened by a purer faith'. The article dealt fairly with some of the chronological and biographical problems associated with Patrick's life, and noted that 'the real St Patrick is very different from the glorified ideal which has bore his name', for the 'lowly, earnest, self-denying evangelist has been surrounded by a halo of hollow and extravagant romance'. The article ended with a call for 'another apostle, like-minded with her "patron saint"' to bring about 'a similar reformation' to what Patrick accomplished in his day. This piece well reveals the way that Evangelicals in the nineteenth century were using Patrick's life to bolster their own theological perspectives.

Among the former he lists the Roman mission of Augustine of Canterbury (died A.D. 604/609); among the latter it is the name of Patrick which receives the most attention: 'Patrick was sent from Scotland to preach to the Irish, who before his time were totally uncivilized, and, some say, cannibals; he however, was useful, and laid the foundations of several churches in Ireland.'[2] While Carey's facts are not entirely correct – the reference to Patrick's Scottish roots, for example is disputable – this statement, along with that from the *Serampore Form of Agreement*, would appear to indicate that the evangelistic success of Patrick and his spiritual heirs in the Celtic church was a source of encouragement to Carey. How much more Carey knew about the historical Patrick is not clear; but he would certainly have

---

2. *An Enquiry into the Obligations of Christians, to Use Means for the Conversion of the Heathens* (Leicester, 1792), p. 32.

been thrilled and inspired by Patrick's evangelistic zeal and God-centred spirituality.

Patrick and Celtic paganism

Given this eighteenth-century memory of Patrick, it is interesting that after Patrick's death, around 460, total silence reigns about him in the Irish Christian tradition until the 630s, when he is mentioned by Cummian (fl. 591–661/2), abbot of Durrow. In a letter to Ségéne (d. 652), abbot of Iona, Cummian describes Patrick as 'holy Patrick, our father'.[3] But this shroud of silence should not be taken to mean that Patrick was forgotten. His works, the *Confession* and the *Letter to the Soldiers of Coroticus*, were obviously cherished, copied and transmitted. Moreover, his missionary labours firmly planted the Christian faith in Irish soil, and left a deep imprint on the Celtic church that would grow up from this soil.

Patrick speaks of 'thousands' converted through his ministry,[4] including sons and daughters of Irish kings.[5] They were converted, he tells us, from the worship of 'idols and filthy things'.[6] It is noteworthy that he here speaks of the worship practices of Celtic paganism with 'scorn and dislike'.[7] On occasions when Patrick was directly confronted by Irish customs that were clearly antithetical to the gospel, he refused to have anything to do with them. For instance, when he came to take passage on the ship to Britain after his escape from captivity, he tells us that he steadfastly refused to suck the breasts of the sailors, for he feared God. To suck the breast of another was an ancient Irish way of declaring one's friendship.[8] Patrick obviously felt that this act was not

3.   Cited R.P.C. Hanson, *Saint Patrick: His Origins and Career* (Oxford: Clarendon Press, 1968), p. 66.

4.   *Confession* 14, 50. See also *Confession* 38; *Letter to the Soldiers of Coroticus* 2.

5.   *Confession* 41–42.

6.   *Confession* 41.

7.   R.P.C. Hanson, *The Life and Writings of the Historical Saint Patrick* (New York, NY: The Seabury Press, 1983), p. 111.

8.   Ludwig Bieler, *Libri Epistolarum Sancti Patricii Episcopi. Part II: Commentary* (Dublin: Stationery Office, 1952), pp. 139-40; R.P.C. Hanson and Cécile Blanc, *Saint Patrick: Confession et Lettre à Coroticus* (Sources chrétiennes, no. 249; Paris: Les Éditions du Cerf, 1978), pp. 34-5 and n.1.

merely a cultural gesture, but was displeasing to God, and while he was prepared to displease the sailors, he was not prepared to anger God. On the same trip, after making landfall in Britain, the pagan sailors found some wild honey after a period of going without food. They dedicated it to a pagan Celtic deity and asked Patrick to partake also. But Patrick recalls, 'Thanks be to God, I tasted none of it.'[9] And right at the very close of his *Confession*, Patrick compares the worship of the elements of this universe with the worship of Christ:

> ...this sun which we see rises daily for us because he [i.e. Christ] commands so, ... what is more, those wretches [*miseri*] who adore it will be painfully punished. Not so we, who believe in, and worship, the true Sun—Christ.[10]

Patrick saw nothing glorious in Celtic idolatry: only a sorry life and a horrific end.

Celtic paganism

Like Graeco-Roman paganism, traditional Celtic religion was profoundly polytheistic, with major deities like Lugh, the sun god (Lugdunum or Lyons in Gaul was named after him, as was Caer Lugubalion or Carlisle), the goddess Brighid, and Cernunnos, the horned god who was a fertility god, and minor deities or guardian spirits who were identified with trees, wells and rivers. A central feature in Celtic paganism were the Druids, who, according to John Sharkey, functioned as 'the custodians of vision and prophecy, sacrifice, poetic lore, the ritual calendar and the law' of the Celtic tribes. Human sacrifice was also a part of Celtic religion. The 1984 discovery of the body of a young man in a peat bog at Lindow in northern England who had been ritually sacrificed two thousand years ago is a stark reminder of the brutal nature of the religion that Patrick's gospel preaching displaced.

---

9.   *Confession* 19, trans. Ludwig Bieler, *The Works of St Patrick, St Secundinus: Hymn on St Patrick* (Ancient Christian Writers, no. 17; 1953 ed.; repr. New York/Ramsey, New Jersey: Paulist Press, n.d.), p. 27.

10. *Confession* 60, trans. Bieler, p. 39, altered.

In order to increase the range of his influence he ordained gospel ministers 'everywhere'.[11] It can be assumed that Patrick trained these men before their ordination. But Patrick gives us no details unless a reference to the sons of kings accompanying him on his evangelistic travels be an allusion to his discipling them.[12] Ultimately, Patrick never loses sight of the fact that it was God's grace that lay behind each and every success of his mission. 'For I am very much God's debtor,' he joyfully confesses, 'who gave me such great grace that many people were reborn in God through me.'[13] There was, in fact, nothing Patrick had by way of abilities that was not God's gift to him.[14]

His missionary labours were not without strong opposition from pagan forces in Ireland. In one section of his *Confession* he says: 'daily I expect murder, fraud, or captivity'.[15] He mentions two distinct occasions of captivity, one for two months and the other for a fortnight.[16] He also relates that he was in peril of death 'twelve' times, though he gives no details of these lest he bore the reader![17] Although Patrick had had status in Roman Britain as the son of a decurion, in Ireland he had no standing at all, for he was a stranger without relatives, and hence without a network of safety and influence. There was no central authority in Ireland, but a multitude of kings – up to 180 or so, it is

11. *Confession* 38, 40, 50.

12. Hanson and Blanc, *Saint Patrick*, p. 125, n.5. Bieler thinks Patrick took these young men with him for protection. See his *The Works of St Patrick, St Secundinus: Hymn on St Patrick* [Ancient Christian Writers, no. 17; 1953 ed.; repr. New York/Ramsey, New Jersey: Paulist Press, n.d.], p. 89, n.114. Clare Stancliffe shares Bieler's view: 'Patrick (*fl.* 5th cent.)', *Oxford Dictionary of National Biography*, Oxford University Press, 2004 (http://www.oxforddnb.com.libaccess.lib.mcmaster.ca/view/article/21562, accessed October 23, 2013).

13. *Confession* 38, trans. Bieler, p. 32. See also *Confession* 46; *Letter to the Soldiers of Coroticus* 11.

14. *Confession* 57.

15. *Confession* 55, trans. Bieler, p. 38.

16. *Confession* 21, 52.

17. *Confession* 35.

reckoned – ruling over various tribes, each of which was bound by ties of blood and patronage (the Old Irish word for these tribes was *túatha*). And to complicate matters further, some of the rulers of smaller tribes owed allegiance to other kings. And to have protection, Patrick had to pay these kings to protect him as he travelled through their lands. He was thus constantly vulnerable to the possibility of personal attack and imprisonment.[18]

Patrick's response to these dangers reveals the true mettle of the man: 'I fear none of these things because of the promises of heaven. I have cast myself into the hands of God Almighty, who rules everywhere, as the prophet says: "Cast thy thought upon God, and he shall sustain thee" (Psalm 55:22).'[19] Later Irish stories about Patrick have him battling druids, the pagan priests of pre-Christian Ireland. Patrick actually never once mentions druids in either his *Confession* or his *Letter to the Soldiers of Coroticus*, though some of the opposition he mentions almost definitely came from them, for they were an extremely powerful body in ancient Irish society. They would have opposed the Christian message that he proclaimed, for it was uncompromising in its condemnation of other religions of the ancient world as idolatry and the veneration of false gods. If people heeded Patrick's preaching, the Druids stood to lose all of their power.[20]

The failure of the Western church to engage in missions

Patrick not only had to face external opposition, though. When Patrick announced his intention in Britain to undertake

---

18. Malcolm Lambert, *Christians and Pagans: The Conversion of Britain from Alban to Bede* (New Haven, CT/London: Yale University Press, 2010), pp. 139, 141; R.P.C. Hanson, 'The Mission of Saint Patrick' in James P. Mackey, ed., *An Introduction to Celtic Christianity* (Edinburgh: T&T Clark, 1989), pp. 35-6.

19. *Confession* 55, trans. Bieler, p. 38.

20. Joseph F.T. Kelly, 'The Attitudes toward Paganism in Early Christian Ireland' in Thomas Halton and Joseph P. Williman, eds., *Diakonia: Studies in Honor of Robert T. Meyer* (Washington, DC: The Catholic University of America Press, 1986), pp. 214-15; Lambert, *Christians and Pagans*, pp. 140-1; Ted Olsen, *Christianity and the Celts* (Downers Grove, IL: InterVarsity Press, 2003), pp. 70-2.

a mission to the Irish there were Christians who strongly opposed him. Patrick recalled their words many years later: 'Many tried to prevent this my mission; they would even talk to each other behind my back and say: "Why does this fellow throw himself into danger among enemies who have no knowledge of God?"'[21] Many of Patrick's Christian contemporaries in the Western Roman Empire appear to have given little thought to evangelizing the 'barbarian' tribes beyond the imperial borders. As Máire B. de Paor notes: 'there was seemingly no organised, concerted effort made to go out and convert pagans, beyond the confines of the Western Roman Empire' during the twilight years of Roman rule in the West.[22] Patrick's mission to Ireland stands in almost splendid isolation in the West. [23]

Typical of this failure to contemplate a mission beyond the imperial realm was Patrick's contemporary, the Gallic theologian Prosper of Aquitaine (c. 390–c. 460). He grapples with various issues about salvation in *The Call of All Nations*. After stating the conviction common to many in the ancient church that the expansion of the Roman Empire was a part of the providential purpose of God to take the gospel to the ends of the earth, Prosper notes: 'the grace of Christianity is not content with the frontiers that are Rome's. Grace has now subjugated to the sceptre of the cross of Christ many peoples whom Rome could not con-

---

21. *Confession* 46, trans. Bieler, p. 36.

22. *Patrick: The Pilgrim Apostle of Ireland*, pp. 23-4.

23. Sometimes the ministry of Ninian, who was based in southern Scotland – see Bede, *Church History* 3.4 – is cited as another exception. But there is good reason to believe that Ninian (Uinniau) needs to be dated in the sixth century. See Thomas Owen Clancy, 'The real St Ninian', *The Innes Review*, 52, no.1 (Spring 2001), pp. 1-28 and Lambert, *Christians and Pagans*, pp. 106-9. For the traditional dating of Ninian, see W. Douglas Simpson, *Saint Ninian and the Origins of the Christian Church in Scotland* (Edinburgh/London: Olive and Boyd, 1940); John Foster, *They Converted Our Ancestors: A Study of the Early Church in Britain* (London: SCM Press, 1965), pp. 30-5; Hanson, *Saint Patrick: His Origins and Career*, pp. 56-63; Charles Thomas, *Christianity in Roman Britain to A.D. 500* (London: Batsford Academic and Educational Ltd., 1981), pp. 275-94.

quer with her arms.'[24] Prosper goes on to observe that there were
some nations 'in the remotest parts of the world' that had not yet
received the gospel. But he was confident that there would come
a time in the future when God would send them the gospel.[25] In
fact, Prosper is aware that some of these nations have received
the gospel through soldiers of these places who have served as
mercenaries in the Roman armies, been converted during their
service for Rome, and then returned home with the Faith.[26]
But he says nothing about plans or strategies to actually take
the gospel to them. It is all left in the lap of God's providence.
And earlier in this work Prosper quotes Matthew 28:19-20 and
Mark 16:15 – both of which Patrick will cite to justify his mission
to the Irish – yet Prosper employs these texts to argue that 'the
gospel of the Cross of Christ was extended to all men without
exception'.[27] On the other hand, what we find in Patrick's *Confession* is paragraph after paragraph on the necessity of engaging
in the task of missions, bespeaking Patrick's uniqueness in his
day.[28] Was it Prosper's stress on the grace of God that dulled his
sense of the necessity of missions?[29]

Mediæval historian Michael Lambert has also found an explanation of this failure of the Western church to evangelize those
beyond the borders of the Empire in the revolutionary change
that occurred in the relationship between the Roman Empire
and the Christian church in the course of the fourth century.[30]

24. Prosper of Aquitaine, *The Call of All Nations* 2.16, trans. P. de Letter, *St Prosper of Aquitaine: The Call of All Nations* (Ancient Christian Writers, no. 14; Westminster, MD: Newman Press/London: Longmans, Green and Co., 1952), p. 120, altered.

25. Prosper of Aquitaine, *The Call of All Nations* 2.17.

26. Prosper of Aquitaine, *The Call of All Nations* 2.33.

27. Prosper of Aquitaine, *The Call of All Nations* 2.2, trans. De Letter, *The Call of All Nations*, pp. 90-1.

28. E.A. Thompson, *Who Was Saint Patrick?* (Woodbridge, Suffolk: The Boydell Press, 1985), pp. 82-3.

29. See Lambert, *Christians and Pagans*, pp. 138-9.

30. Lambert, *Christians and Pagans*, p. 138.

The acclamation of Constantine (c. 285–337) as emperor in the Western Roman Empire at York in 306 and his subsequent reign of thirty-one years necessitated a fundamental change in Christians' perspective about the Empire, for Constantine not only secured legal toleration for Christianity but his actions also bespoke a conviction that he had been called by God to be the Church's patron.

The legislation enacted by Constantine and those texts that we have from his hand reveal a man who was sincerely convinced that he had been given a divine mission to inculcate virtue in his subjects and persuade them to worship the true God proclaimed in the Christian faith. This conviction was wedded to an intense ambition for personal power, but that does not diminish its sincerity.[31] Fourth-century Christian leaders thus found themselves having to re-evaluate their understanding of the role of the Roman Empire in history.[32]

Prior to the Constantinian revolution, Rome had been the great persecutor of the church. Thus, a Christian author like the North African theologian Tertullian was certain that Rome was like Babylon of old: this ancient Near Eastern imperial capital is the best 'metaphor of the Roman city,' he said, since, 'like Babylon, [Rome] is great, and proud of empire, and at war against the saints of God.'[33] One of the earliest texts in Latin that relates to Christianity is an official record of the trial of some believers from Scillium, a town in the Roman province of Numidia in

---

31. Vital in orienting my perspective on Constantine has been Timothy D. Barnes, *Constantine and Eusebius* (Cambridge, MA/London: Harvard University Press, 1981). For a concise study of this question, see also my 'Constantine and his Revolution', *The Fellowship for Reformation and Pastoral Studies*, 27, no.6 (February, 1999).

32. For studies of this re-orientation, see W.H.C. Frend, 'The Roman Empire in Eastern and Western Historiography' in his *Religion Popular and Unpopular in the Early Christian Centuries* (London: Variorum Reprints, 1976), no. IX; R. A. Markus, 'The Roman Empire in Early Christian Historiography' in his *From Augustine to Gregory the Great: History and Christianity in Late Antiquity* (London: Variorum Reprints, 1983), no. IV.

33. *Against Marcion* 3.13, trans. Ernest Evans, *Tertullian: Adversus Marcionem* (Oxford: Clarendon Press, 1972), p. 211.

North Africa, around the year 180. It contains a similar view of
Rome to that of Tertullian. Speratus, one of a number who was
martyred for the faith on that occasion, is recorded as telling the
Proconsul of Africa: 'I do not recognize the empire of this world;
instead, I serve that God whom no man sees nor can see with
these eyes.'[34]

After the accession of Constantine, however, Christianity
was in a favoured position of power, and Christian authors had
to re-evaluate their position vis-à-vis Rome. For much of the
fourth century it was the re-evaluation espoused by Eusebius of
Caesarea (c. 260–c. 339), sometimes called the father of church
history, which seems to have prevailed in many circles.[35] Eusebius argued that the establishment of the *pax Romana* under the
imperial rule of Augustus Caesar (63 B.C.–A.D. 14) was a direct
fulfilment of Scripture texts like Psalm 72:7-8, Isaiah 2:4, and
Micah 5:4-5, which predicted political peace at the time of the
coming of the Messiah.[36] Constantine's similar political achievement, coupled with an overt commitment to the advance of the
Christian faith, marked out his reign as another high point in
God's providential purposes in the history of the Roman Empire. Eusebius thus ends his famous narrative of the history of
the church on a high note of optimism, for Constantine had

34. *Acts of the Scillitan Martyrs* in Robert M. Grant, ed., *Second-Century Christianity:
A Collection of Fragments* (2nd ed.; Louisville/London: Westminster John Knox
Press, 2003), p. 47, altered.

35. For helpful summaries of Eusebius's view, see Frend, 'Roman Empire in Eastern
and Western Historiography', pp. 27-8; Markus, 'Roman Empire in Early Christian Historiography', pp. 343-4; Glenn F. Chesnut, Jr., 'The Patterns of the Past:
Augustine's debate with Eusebius and Sallust' in John Deschner, Leroy T. Howe,
and Klaus Penzel, eds., *Our Common History as Christians. Essays in Honor of Albert
C. Outler* (New York: Oxford University Press, 1975), pp. 69-95, *passim*; Avihu Zakai and Anya Mali, 'Time, History and Eschatology: Ecclesiastical History from
Eusebius to Augustine', *The Journal of Religious History*, 17 (1993), pp. 393-402. For
a new collection of essays on various aspects of Eusebius's thought, see especially
Aaron Johnson and Jeremy Schott, eds., *Eusebius of Caesarea: Tradition and Innova-
tions* (Cambridge, MA/London: Center for Hellenic Studies, 2013).

36. *The Preparation for the Gospel* 1.4; *The Proof of the Gospel* 7.2.

'combined the Roman Empire into a single whole, as in former days' – a reference to the Augustan achievement – and brought it all under his 'peaceful rule, from the rising of the sun to the farthest dark'.[37] Laws were now passed that 'reflected liberality and true piety', so that, in Eusebius's glowing prose,

> all tyranny was eradicated, and the kingdom that was theirs was preserved, secure and undisputed, for Constantine and his sons alone. They, having first cleansed the world of hatred to God and knowing all the good he had conferred on them, showed their love of virtue and of God, their devotion and gratitude to the Almighty, by their actions for all to see.[38]

Implicit in these historical reflections is the view that God's providential guidance of history had reached its zenith in the Christian Roman Empire and that the Empire was critical in the extension of Christ's kingdom.[39] As Lambert notes, it follows that 'the proper place for spreading the Gospel lay among the peoples within the Empire rather than outside.'[40] Reinforcing this conviction was the long-standing disdain Romans had had for non-Roman peoples, 'the barbarians', and also, with regard to specifically the Irish, the fact that Irish pirates were raiding at will Romano-British settlements.[41]

Behind Patrick's missional passion

Patrick thus stands as a major innovator in his day. Like Paul in the apostolic era, or William Carey at the fountain-head of the modern missionary movement, Patrick was constrained to spend his life in missions, in particular, the evangelization of the Irish. A concern for the salvation of pagans manifested itself not long

---

37. *Church History* 10.9, trans. Paul L. Maier, *Eusebius: The Church History* (Grand Rapids, MI: Kregel, 1999), p. 370.

38. *Church History* 10.9, trans. Maier, p. 371.

39. Zakai and Mali, *Time, History and Eschatology*, pp. 399-401.

40. Lambert, *Christians and Pagans*, p. 138.

41. ibid.

after his conversion. When he took ship to a Britain after his escape from slavery, he hoped that his refusal to engage in the pagan Irish custom of sucking the breast, mentioned above, would lead the sailors to 'the faith of Jesus Christ'.[42] A major turning-point in his life, though, came a few years later when he received what he regarded as a personal call to go back to Ireland as an evangelist:

> [A]fter a few years I was in Britain with my people, who received me as their son, and sincerely besought me that now at last, having suffered so many hardships, I should not leave them and go elsewhere.
>
> And there I saw in the night the vision of a man, whose name was Victoricus, coming as it were from Ireland, with countless letters. And he gave me one of them, and I read the opening words of the letter, which were, 'The voice of the Irish'; and as I read the beginning of the letter I thought that at the same moment I heard their voice – they were those beside the Wood of Voclut, which is near the Western Sea – and thus did they cry out as with one mouth: 'We ask thee, boy, come and walk among us once more.'
>
> And I was quite broken in heart, and could read no further, and so I woke up. Thanks be to God, after many years the Lord gave to them according to their cry.[43]

As we have noted, Patrick did not immediately leave Britain to go to Ireland. It was 'after many years,' to use his words, that he actually was able to return to Ireland. If he escaped from captivity around 412, he did not return to Ireland till about 430. So the passage of time between his personal call as laid out in this vision and his stepping foot again on Irish soil may well have been close to twenty years.

During this time, as mentioned already in Chapter 1, Patrick was acquiring a profound knowledge of the Scriptures. And as he

---

42. *Confession* 18.

43. *Confession* 23, trans. Bieler, p. 28.

did so, this personal call was confirmed by Scripture after Scripture in which God called upon his people to take the knowledge of Christ to the nations that dwelt in spiritual darkness.

> I am very much God's debtor, who gave me such grace that many people were reborn in God through me and afterwards confirmed, and that clergy were ordained for them everywhere, for a people just coming to the faith, whom the Lord took from the utmost parts of the earth, as he once had promised through his prophets: 'To you the Gentiles shall come from the ends of the earth and shall say: "How false are the idols that our fathers got for themselves, and there is no profit in them"';[44] and again: 'I have set you as a light among the Gentiles, that you may be for their salvation to the end of the earth.'[45]

> And there I wish to wait for his promise who surely never deceives, as he promises in the Gospel: 'They shall come from the east and the west, and shall sit down with Abraham and Isaac and Jacob'[46] — as we believe the faithful will come from all the world.

> We ought to fish well and diligently, as the Lord exhorts in advance and teaches, saying: 'Come after me, and I will make you fishers of men.'[47] And again he says through the prophets: 'Behold, I send many fishers and hunters, says God,' and so on.[48] Hence it was most necessary to spread our nets so that a great multitude and throng might be caught for God, and that there be clergy everywhere to baptize and exhort a people in need and want, as the Lord in the Gospel states, exhorts and teaches, saying: 'Going therefore now, teach all nations, baptizing them in the name of the Father, and the Son, and the Holy Spirit, teaching them to observe all things, whatever I have commanded you: and behold I am with you all days even

---

44. Jeremiah 16:19
45. Acts 13:47, citing Isaiah 49:6
46. Matthew 8:11
47. Matthew 4:19
48. Jeremiah 16:16

to the consummation of the world.'[49] And again he says: 'Go therefore into the whole world, and preach the Gospel to every creature. He that believes and is baptized shall be saved; but he that believes not shall be condemned.'[50] And again: 'This Gospel of the kingdom shall be preached in the whole world for a testimony to all nations, and then the end shall come.'[51] And so too the Lord announces through the prophet, and says: 'And it shall come to pass, in the last days, says the Lord, I will pour out of my Spirit upon all flesh; and your sons and your daughters shall prophesy, and your young men shall see visions, and your old men shall dream dreams. And upon my servants indeed, and upon my handmaids will I pour out in those days of my Spirit, and they shall prophesy.'[52] And in Hosea, he says: 'I will call that which was not my people, my people; and her that had not obtained mercy, one that has obtained mercy. And it shall be in the place where it was said: "You are not my people," there they shall be called the sons of the living God.'[53]

This piling of Scripture text upon Scripture text is typical among early Christian writers.[54] Prosper of Aquitaine, for example, whose thought on missions we looked at earlier in this chapter, has a similar listing of texts in his *The Call of All Nations* as he seeks to demonstrate that the salvation of God is for all nations.[55] The stress on the gospel going to the 'ends of the earth' in some of the texts that Patrick cites also reinforced his conviction about the necessity of taking the gospel to the Irish, for, as far as he knew, the Irish inhabited the final piece of land at the world's furthest extremity. Beyond Ireland was nothing but the vast watery expanse of the

49. Matthew 28:19-20

50. Mark 16:15-16

51. Matthew 24:14

52. Acts 2:17-18, citing Joel 2:28-29

53. *Confession* 38–40, trans. Bieler, pp. 33-4, altered. The final quote is from Romans 9:25-26, citing Hosea 1:10; 2:1, 23.

54. Christine Mohrmann, *The Latin of Saint Patrick* (Dublin: Dublin Institute for Advanced Studies, 1961), p. 41.

55. Prosper of Aquitaine, *The Call of All Nations* 2.18.

Atlantic Ocean, 'the Western Sea,' as Patrick called it.[56] In Patrick's mind, he had been given the incredible privilege of preaching Christianity to the literally last nation to be evangelized.[57] And this added even more to Patrick's wonder at God's grace: that he, an unlearned man, should be chosen to take the gospel to the final people on the earth who needed to hear it. As he said:

> Who am I, O Lord, or what is my calling, that you have worked together with me with such divine power, so that to-day I constantly exalt and magnify your name among the nations (*in gentibus*) wherever I may be, not only in good days but also in tribulations? So whatever happens to me, be it good or evil, I ought always to accept it and give thanks to God, who showed me that I can trust him always without any doubts, and who must have heard my prayer so that I, however ignorant (*inscius*) I was, in the last days dared to undertake such a holy and wonderful work— thus imitating somehow those who, as the Lord once foretold, would preach his Gospel for a testimony to all nations before the end of the world. So we have seen it, and so it has been fulfilled: indeed, we are witnesses that the Gospel has been preached unto those parts beyond which there lives nobody.[58]

As this text also makes clear and as we have already noted in Chapter 2, Patrick was convinced he was living at the close of history, for in evangelizing the Irish, he had taken the gospel to the very last people without the knowledge of Christ. As Hanson observes: 'It is remarkable that one who thought there would be almost no future for the world should in fact have labored with such success that he laid the foundations of Irish Christianity' for generations to come.[59]

---

56. *Confession* 23. See also Hanson, 'Mission of Saint Patrick' in Mackey, ed., *Introduction to Celtic Christianity*, p. 34; idem, *Life and Writings of the Historical Saint Patrick*, p. 23: 'To a man of classical antiquity, [Ireland] was literally the last country on earth. It was the most westerly country in Europe; beyond it was nothing.'

57. Philip Freeman, *St Patrick of Ireland. A Biography* (New York: Simon & Schuster, 2004), pp. 119-25.

58. *Confession* 34, trans. Bieler, p. 31, altered.

59. Hanson, 'Mission of Saint Patrick' in Mackey, ed., *Introduction to Celtic Christianity*, p. 35. See also Lambert, *Christians and Pagans*, p. 140.

The growth of Christianity

Sociologist Rodney Stark has estimated that Christianity grew in the first three centuries of its existence from roughly a few thousand believers c. A.D. 40, comprising .0017 per cent of the population of the Roman Empire – based on an estimated population of 60 million – to over 6,000,000 by 300, roughly 10.5 per cent of the total population, assuming the size of the population remained fairly stable. During the fourth century, this percentage of professing Christians increased even further, although the fact that Christianity became the only legal religion in this era has to be taken into account in this growth.

Why such growth? Well, there was the power of the Scriptures to convert its readers—Patrick's own devotion to the Bible certainly is linked to this. There was also the power of the actual message of the Christian gospel, which, in the words of early Church historian Henry Chadwick, 'spoke of divine grace in Christ, the remission of sins and the conquest of evil powers for the sick soul, tired of living and scared of dying, seeking for an assurance of immortality and for security and freedom in a world where the individual could rarely do other than submit to his fate.'

A further reason for cross-cultural evangelism was that Patrick's own conversion gave him a deep sense of gratitude to God, and out of thanks to God he felt bound to go back to Ireland and preach the good news of saving grace in Christ:

> I cannot be silent – nor, indeed, is it expedient – about the great benefits and the great grace which the Lord has deigned to bestow upon me in 'the land of my captivity';[60] for this is what we can give back to God after having been chastened and having come to know him, to exalt and praise his wonders before every nation that is under the whole heaven.[61]

Patrick's mission to the Irish was also rooted in his love for the Irish people. As he stated at the very outset of his letter to the soldiers of the warlord Coroticus, 'out of love for my neighbours and sons I have given up my country and parents and my life to

---

60.   cf. 2 Chronicles 6:37

61.   *Confession* 3, trans. Bieler, pp. 21-2, altered.

the point of death'.[62] Later in the letter Patrick refers to the fact that these men were contemptuous of the Irish: 'For them it is a disgrace that we are Irish.'[63] What is noteworthy about this statement is that Patrick's love for those to whom he had preached the good news had led to his being willing to identify himself with them. There had been a time, Patrick admitted, when such love was utterly foreign to his character. But God dealt with him in mercy and love, and so transformed his character that he was happy to 'care and labour for the salvation' of the Irish.[64]

Then, a desire to see God glorified had compelled him to engage in mission:

> Did I come to Ireland without God, or according to the flesh? Who compelled me? I am bound by the Spirit (*alligatus sum Spiritu*) not to see any of my kinsfolk. Is it of my own doing that I have holy mercy on the people who once took me captive and made away with the servants and maids of my father's house? I was freeborn according to the flesh. I am the son of a decurion. But I sold my noble rank – I am neither ashamed nor sorry – for the good of others. Thus I am a slave (*servus*) in Christ to a foreign nation for the unspeakable glory of 'life everlasting which is in Christ Jesus our Lord'.[65]

It would appear from this text that Patrick used his own finances, inherited most likely from his parents in Britain, to fund his mission. As has been mentioned, for example, he often had to pay the various Irish kings for protection as he travelled through their lands in Ireland.[66] As a result he impoverished himself.

The statement 'I am bound by the Spirit (*alligatus sum Spiritu*)' in this passage also occurs in the *Confession*:

---

62. *Letter to the Soldiers of Coroticus* 1, trans. Bieler, p. 41.

63. *Confession* 16, trans. Bieler, p. 45.

64. *Confession* 28.

65. *Letter to the Soldiers of Coroticus* 10, trans. Bieler, pp. 43-4, altered. For the quote, cf. Romans 6:23.

66. *Confession* 51–53.

Wherefore, then, even if I wished to leave ... and go to Britain
– and how I would have loved to go to my country and my
parents, and also to Gaul in order to visit the brethren and to
see the face of the saints of my Lord! God knows it that I much
desired it; but I am bound by the Spirit (*alligatus Spiritu*) who
gives evidence against me if I do this, telling me that I shall be
guilty; and I am afraid of losing the labour which I have begun
– nay, not I, but Christ the Lord who bade me come here and
stay with them for the rest of my life, if the Lord will.[67]

The phrase is drawn directly from Acts 20:22, where the apostle
Paul tells the Ephesian elders that he is 'bound in the Spirit'
(King James Version) to go to Jerusalem, despite the probabil-
ity that he would experience much suffering there. Paul is committed to doing what he perceives as God's will, no matter the
cost. The clear implication in Patrick's use of this term is that he
shares the apostle's attitude and depth of commitment. As he
also commented:

I came to the people of Ireland to preach the Gospel, and to
suffer insult from the unbelievers, bearing the reproach of my
going abroad and many persecutions even unto bonds, and to
give my free birth for the benefit of others; and, should I be
worthy, I am prepared to give even my life without hesitation
and most gladly for his name, and it is there that I wish to spend
it until I die, if the Lord would grant it to me.[68]

Taken together, all these texts regarding the mission to the Irish
reveal a man who has absolute certainty of God's deep desire
for the nations to hear the Gospel and also of God's specific
purposes for his life. And so Patrick was prepared to live out his
days in Ireland that the Irish might come to know the Triune
God as he had done.

---

67. *Confession* 43, trans. Bieler, p. 35. For further discussion of the phrase 'bound by
the Spirit', see Chapter 4.

68. *Confession* 37, trans. Bieler, p. 32.

Patrick's missional legacy

While the course of Patrick's travels in Ireland is not at all clear from his *Confession*, they were probably restricted to the northern half of the island, to Ulster and North Connaught.[69] In human terms, his ministry was extremely successful, though he certainly had not evangelized the whole of the north of Ireland by the time of his death, which cannot have been long after he wrote his *Confession*.[70] His final days, though, were ones of trouble.

The romance and reality of the Celtic church

In the second half of the nineteenth century a Gaelic-speaking Scottish Baptist by the name of William Fraser argued that the Celtic church had 'no connections with the state' and as such it was 'more simple, pure and scriptural in faith and practice' than any other Christian body in late antiquity (500–700). This romantic portrait of the Celtic church probably tells us more about Fraser – he was an independent-minded Baptist – than about the real nature of Celtic Christianity. The latter was definitely a product of Patrick's ministry and shared to the full his passion for the Scriptures, his Trinitarianism, and his zeal for evangelism.

Yet, the Celtic church also had a rigorous ascetic strain – some of its monks followed the solitary model favoured by Egyptian and Syrian monks rather than the communal Benedictine model followed by continental monks in Western Europe. One of the most remarkable monasteries in the Celtic world is that built on a ledge 550 feet up the side of Skellig Michael, a remote island off the coast of County Kerry. Here the monks had to live on a diet of fish and puffins, and were exposed to all of the elements of the Atlantic Ocean. Sharing Patrick's view of Ireland as being at the end of the world, the monks here would have regarded themselves as living at the very edge of that very last land, the place where sky, sea, and land meet – for them, an ideal place for solitary prayer and contemplation.

---

69. Lambert, *Christians and Pagans*, p. 146.

70. Thompson, *Who Was Saint Patrick?* pp. 84-5. Patrick was an old man when he wrote his *Confession*. See *Confession* 62: 'This is my confession before I die' (trans. Bieler, *Works of St Patrick*, p. 40).

Despite the evident success of Patrick's ministry, charges were levelled against Patrick that resurrected a sin of his youth before his conversion and that accused him of having undertaken the mission to Ireland for the basest of reasons, namely financial gain.[71] Patrick's *Confession* was written in part to lay these criticisms and charges to rest once and for all.[72]

The Celtic church in Ireland definitely inherited Patrick's missionary zeal. His spiritual descendants, men like Columba (c. 521–597), Columbanus (c. 543–615), and Aidan (d. 651), partook of this missionary fervour, so that the Celtic church became, in the words of James Carney, 'a reservoir of spiritual vigour, which would ... fructify the parched lands of western Europe'.[73] It is surely no coincidence that what was prominent in Patrick's life was reproduced in the lives of his heirs.[74]

71. *Confession* 26–32. See also *Confession* 49–55, where Patrick speaks about his integrity when it came to money matters.

72. Thompson, *Who Was Saint Patrick?*, pp. 144-6; Máire B. de Paor, *Patrick: The Pilgrim Apostle of Ireland* (New York, NY: Regan Books, 1998), pp. 145-52; Freeman, *St Patrick of Ireland*, pp. 142-9.

73. James Carney, 'Sedulius Scottus' in Robert McNally, ed., *Old Ireland* (New York, NY: Fordham University Press 1965), p. 230.

74. Diarmuid Ó Laoghaire 'Old Ireland and Her Spirituality' in McNally, ed., *Old Ireland*, p. 33. See also Hanson, 'Mission of Saint Patrick' in Mackey, ed., *Introduction to Celtic Christianity*, pp. 43-4; Lambert, *Christians and Pagans*, p. 147.

4

'GOD HAS SPOKEN':
Word and Spirit in Patrick's Piety

'God has spoken'

Despite the protestations of his rusticity, words – Latin, Old Irish, and his native British tongue – must have been deeply important to Patrick, for they were central to his calling as an evangelist. They were also the means by which God spoke to him in the Holy Scriptures. Apart from these words from God, and the credal statement that we looked at in Chapter 2, we cannot be sure of any other books that Patrick had read.[1] But one thing we do know: Patrick knew his Bible.

Like the Christian Faith throughout the Patristic era, Patrick's religion was bibliocentric – it was centred around Scriptures, the Old Testament and what Origen had termed the 'so-called New Testament'.[2] By the late fourth century, battles with regard to the canon – particularly intense in the second century with the Church's fight against the heretical Gnostics and their false gospels, on the one hand, and against the schismatic Montanists and their fresh words of prophecy, on the other – were essen-

---

1. However, see P. Dronke, 'St Patrick's reading', *Cambridge Medieval Celtic Studies*, 1 (1981), pp. 21-38. See also Colmán Etchingham, 'Preface to the Paperback Edition' of E.A. Thompson, *Who Was Saint Patrick?* (Woodbridge, Suffolk: Boydell Press, 1999), pp. xxvi–xxvii.

2. Origen, *Commentary on John* 5:8.

tially over. This was because the church in both the eastern and western Mediterranean came to a solid agreement about the shape of the New Testament canon that consists of the identical twenty-seven books found in Bibles today.[3]

Gnosticism and Montanism

The determination of the New Testament canon in the second century was shaped to a great degree by the necessity of responding to the heresy of Gnosticism, on the one hand, and the schismatic Montanists, on the other. Rooted in a cosmological dualism that regarded the material world as inherently evil and the realm of spirit as good, Gnostics generally rejected the Old Testament that clearly spoke of God as Creator and accepted only selected portions of the New Testament. The Gnostics also created their own holy books such as *The Gospel of Thomas* and *The Gospel of Philip*. While the Montanists upheld the canon, they were open to the possibility of fresh words of revelation being given by the Holy Spirit. Nearly all of these fresh words had to do with ethical issues like marriage and church discipline. The church was thus compelled to recognize the full extent of the boundaries of the New Testament and also to affirm unequivocally that the canon had been closed since the end of the apostolic era.

Patrick is an heir of this agreement regarding the extent of the New Testament canon. While he complains that he does not know the Scriptures like other learned men, and that he cannot express himself like such gifted speakers,[4] the truth of the matter is that his two works reveal a man who has immersed himself in the Scriptures. As Malcolm Lambert rightly puts it: 'at the heart of the *Confessio* lies a sophisticated mosaic of scriptural texts and references deployed with great skill'.[5]

---

3.   Joseph T. Kelly, 'Christianity and the Latin Tradition in Early Medieval Ireland', *Bulletin of The John Rylands University Library of Manchester*, 68, no.2 (Spring 1986), pp. 411-13.

4.   *Confession* 9–10.

5.   *Christians and Pagans: The Conversion of Britain from Alban to Bede* (New Haven, CT/ London: Yale University Press, 2010), p. 143.

Patrick introduces citations and quotations from the Bible with a variety of phrases. For instance, there is 'the Lord says' or 'the Lord promises',[6] — clear indications that Patrick viewed Scripture as a word coming from the mouth of God. He uses both of these introductory phrases in the long string of biblical quotations regarding mission cited in the previous chapter (*Confession* 39-40). This series of quotations ground the mission to the Irish in Scriptural injunction and command. Sometimes he uses a phrase that indicates Scripture itself speaks: 'Scripture says'.[7] Other times, he employs a standard biblical and Patristic phrase, 'it is written'.[8] A few times he recognizes a human author as the speaker of the biblical text.[9]

As to the text that Patrick employs, it is generally what is called the Old Latin version.[10] This version consists of a multitude of Latin copies of the Scriptures produced between the second and fourth centuries. The first of these probably appeared in the late second century, when it appears that Christians in North Africa produced the first Latin version of the New Testament.[11] In the 380s the Christian author Jerome (c. 345-420), living at the time in Rome, began work on a definitive translation known as the Vulgate, which in time would completely replace the Old Latin version and become the definitive Latin text of the Bible. Given Patrick's relative isolation in Ireland, it is not surprising that most

---

6. *Confession* 5, 7, 29, 38, 39, 40 (six times this phrase or something similar is used); *Letter to the Soldiers of Coroticus* 18.

7. *Confession* 9, 11; *Letter to the Soldiers of Coroticus* 14, 15.

8. *Confession* 11, 20, 48; *Letter to the Soldiers of Coroticus* 11, 16.

9. *Confession* 23 (the apostle Paul), 55 (the Psalmist— 'the prophet says'); *Letter to the Soldiers of Coroticus* 18 (the apostle Peter). See Ludwig Bieler, *Libri Epistolarum Sancti Patricii Episcopi. Part II: Commentary* (Dublin: Stationery Office, 1952), p. 107.

10. For the following discussion of the text of Patrick's Latin Bible, see Ludwig Bieler, 'Der bibletext des heiligen Patrick', *Biblica*, 28 (1947), pp. 31-58, 236-63. See also the review of this article in *Studies: An Irish Quarterly Review*, 36, no.143 (September 1947), pp. 370-3.

11. Bruce M. Metzger, *The Early Versions of the New Testament: Their Origin, Transmission and Limitations* (Oxford: Clarendon Press, 1977), pp. 288-90.

of his citations of the Scriptures are from the Old Latin version. His use of the Vulgate is extremely limited. His seven quotations or citations from Acts, for example, all come from Jerome's Vulgate, but when he cites the Gospels, most of the citations are from the Old Latin, though a few do come from the Vulgate.

Among the Gospels, Matthew is by far Patrick's favourite from which to quote or cite. He has at least twelve citations or quotations from Matthew, as compared to three apiece from Mark and John, and only two from Luke. The writings of Paul are another favourite — roughly forty citations or quotes, nearly a third of all his biblical references. Curiously, there are about a dozen biblical citations for which there is no known Old Latin text.

We get an important insight into Patrick's view of the Scriptures in his *Letter to the Soldiers of Coroticus*. As he draws the letter to a close, Patrick wishes to emphasize that his condemnation of the actions of Coroticus's warriors is not simply his own personal judgment. Rather, it corresponds to God's deep displeasure at what these men had done. In Patrick's words:

> It is not my words that I have set forth in Latin, but those of God and the apostles and the prophets, who have never lied. 'He who believes shall be saved; but he who believes not shall be condemned.'[12] 'God has spoken.'[13]

The words of 'God and the apostles and the prophets,' namely the words of Scripture he has cited or alluded to in the letter, will not deceive the reader. Patrick then cites most of Mark 16:16 - which follows the Markan version of the Great Commission - to encourage repentance on the part of his readers. He closes with a citation from either Psalm 60:6a or 108:7, which reinforces the truthfulness of the text from Mark and forms a fitting commentary on all of the

---

12. Mark 16:16

13. *Letter to the Soldiers of Coroticus* 20, trans. Ludwig Bieler, *The Works of St Patrick, St Secundinus: Hymn on St Patrick* [Ancient Christian Writers, no. 17; 1953 ed.; repr. New York/Ramsey, New Jersey: Paulist Press, n.d.], pp. 46-7, altered.

biblical passages referred to in the epistle.[14] This final phrase, 'God has spoken', bears out the observation made by John Carey about Patrick's piety: it is marked by 'his passionate fidelity to the letter of the Scriptures, his conviction that the Bible is an expression of absolute truth beyond the possibility of qualification or compromise'.[15]

Prayer and the Spirit

Máire de Paor makes the apt observation that the Holy Spirit 'pervades and illuminates [Patrick's] entire *Confessio'*.[16] Patrick especially links his prayer life to the Holy Spirit. For Patrick, it is the Spirit who provides the energy for him to maintain a life of prayer and so fulfill 1 Thessalonians 5:17, 'Pray continually'. Patrick found that daily prayer is a key means of divine encouragement in times of blessing and times of adversity. Moreover, as we shall see, what he says about the Spirit and prayer is guided by the Scriptures as the interpretive guide for all of his experiences.

Fourth-century thinking about the Spirit

The fourth century was a great age for reflection on the person and work of the Holy Spirit. In some ways, this was a result of the rise of monasticism as well as the fight against the denial of the Spirit's deity in the Arian controversy. Patrick's emphasis on the Spirit as the Spirit of grace and mission fits well with other writings such as: Basil of Caesarea's biblical defence of the deity of the Holy Spirit in *On the Holy Spirit* (375), Augustine's remarkable reflections of the Spirit as the bond of love between God the Father and God the Son in his *On the Trinity* (399–c. 420), and the rich study of the Spirit and spiritual warfare in homilies of Macarius, a Syrian monk (between 380–410).

---

14. See Richard P.C. Hanson and Cécile Blanc, *Saint Patrick: Confession et Lettre à Coroticus* (Sources Chrétiennes, no. 249; Paris: Les Éditions du Cerf, 1978), p. 152, n. 1.

15. 'Saint Patrick, the Druids, and the End of the World', *History of Religions*, 36 (1996), p. 52.

16. Máire B. de Paor, *Patrick: The Pilgrim Apostle of Ireland* (New York, NY: Regan Books, 1998), p. 97. See also Noel Dermot O'Donoghue, *Aristocracy of Soul: Patrick of Ireland* (Wilmington, DE: Michael Glazier, 1987), p. 43; John Carey, 'Saint Patrick, the Druids, and the End of the World', *History of Religions*, 36 (1996), p. 50.

The first mention of prayer and the Holy Spirit is in a context marked by adversity. Taken captive to Ireland, Patrick filled his days with prayer while tending sheep. These times of solitude provided times of respite for him, so much so, he would 'say as many as a hundred prayers' in the day, and 'almost as many in the night'.[17] These times of prayer were so fruitful because, he later realized, the Spirit was fervently working within him.

> But after I came to Ireland – every day I had to tend sheep, many times a day I prayed – the love of God and his fear came to me more and more, and my faith was strengthened. And my spirit was moved so that in a single day I would say as many as a hundred prayers, and almost as many in the night, and this even when I was staying in the woods and on the mountain; and I used to get up for prayer before daylight, through snow, through frost, through rain, and I felt no harm, and there was no sloth in me – as I now see, because the Spirit within me was then fervent.[18]

The indwelling ministry of the Spirit made Patrick diligent, despite the rigorous living conditions. No amount of arduous surroundings – whether rain, snow, or frost – deterred his piety, for the Holy Spirit moved the spirit of Patrick to devote himself to prayer. In like fashion, Paul exhorts the Roman church with similar exhortations: 'Do not be slothful in diligence, be fervent in the Spirit, serve the Lord, rejoice in hope, endure tribulation, be devoted to prayer.'[19] The Holy Spirit sustained Patrick's life of prayer, and as a result of constant prayer, 'the love of God and his fear came to me more and more, and my faith was strengthened'. Patrick's hundreds of prayers, prompted by the indwelling Spirit, strengthened him to rise early in the morning and live a life devoted to prayer.

Prompted by the voice of God, as we have seen, Patrick later fled from slavery and set out for a boat some two hundred miles away that was to sail for Britain. Upon his arrival, the captain in-

---

17. *Confession* 16, trans. Bieler, p. 25.

18. *Confession* 16, trans. Bieler, p. 25, altered.

19. Romans 12:11-12, trans. Shawn J. Wilhite.

itially refused to allow Patrick to go onto the boat. Patrick turned
back and began praying. As he recounts, 'and before I had ended
my prayer, I heard one of them shouting behind me, "Come,
hurry, we shall take you on in good faith"'.[20] When confronted
with roadblocks, Patrick turned to prayer.

Upon arriving in Britain, Patrick recalls an evening when Satan assailed him. Patrick and the sailors are now travelling by
foot after their journey from Ireland. They are without food and
are growing restless. But in the providence of God, a herd of
pigs come across their path and the sailors are able to kill some
and fill their stomachs.[21] That evening, though, Patrick tells how
'Satan assailed me violently.'[22] It was so vivid for Patrick that
he comments that he will remember this experience 'as long as
I shall be in this body'. Satan falls on Patrick, as he retells the
incident, like a huge rock, rendering him immobile. Upon seeing the sun rise that morning, however, Patrick shouts out 'Helias! Helias!' and is immediately freed from the demonic attack.
Scholars have long debated what this could mean: did Patrick
actually call on the Sun-god Helios? Recent study has shown,
however, that rather than observing some form of pagan Irish
custom of calling on the Sun, there is good evidence that Patrick
seems to be echoing Christ's words on the cross, as recorded by
Mark: 'Eloi, Eloi, lama sabachthani' (Mark 15:34).[23] During this
trial, Patrick credits Christ with sustaining him and the Spirit
with inspiring him to call forth in prayer to the true God.

> And I believe that I was sustained by Christ my Lord, and that
> his Spirit was even then crying out on my behalf, and I hope

---

20. *Confession* 18, trans. Bieler, p. 26.

21. *Confession* 19.

22. *Confession* 20, trans. Bieler, p. 27.

23. See Patrick Skehan, 'St Patrick and Elijah' in Pierre Casetti, Othmar Keel and Adri-
     an Schenker, eds., *Mélanges Dominique Barthélemy: Études bibliques offertes à l'occasion
     de son 60ᵉ anniversaire* (Fribourg, Switzerland: Éditions Universitaires/Göttingen:
     Vandenhoeck & Ruprecht, 1981), pp. 471-83.

it will be so 'on the day of my tribulation',[24] as is written in the Gospel: 'On that day,' the Lord declares, 'it is not you that speaks, but the Spirit of your Father that speaks in you.'[25]

Here Patrick has a partial allusion to Psalm 50:15 but a clear quotation of Matthew 10:20. When Jesus sends out the twelve apostles (Matt. 10:5), he promises the Spirit will speak through them when they are brought before officials and rulers (Matt. 10:16-23). Patrick is asserting that Jesus's promise of the Spirit's help was realized in his own life when the Spirit prayed and cried out on his behalf during this day of battle with Satan.

In another vision Patrick mentions yet again the Spirit in relation to his life of prayer. As Patrick recalled this vision, he remembered seeing someone praying within his body and heard him praying above his inner man. This 'person' was praying powerfully with deep-seated groans; eventually he revealed himself to be none other than the Holy Spirit.

> And again I saw him praying in me, and I was as it were within my body, and I heard him above me, that is, over the inward man, and there he prayed mightily with groanings. And all the time I was astonished, and wondered, and thought with myself who it could be that prayed in me. But at the end of the prayer he spoke, saying that he was the Spirit; and so I woke up, and remembered the apostle saying: 'The Spirit helps the infirmities of our prayer. For we know not what we should pray for as we ought; but the Spirit himself asks for us with unspeakable groanings, which cannot be expressed in words';[26] and again: 'The Lord our advocate asks for us.'[27]

On waking up, Patrick immediately remembered two portions of Scripture that to him validated his experience: Romans 8:26 and 1 John 2:1. The Romans text is a unique passage in Holy

---

24. Psalm 50:15

25. *Confession* 20, trans. Bieler, p. 27, citing Matthew 10:20.

26. Romans 8:26

27. *Confession* 25, trans. Bieler, pp. 28-9, altered. At the close of this text, Patrick is thinking of 1 John 2:1.

Scripture where Paul states that the Spirit actively prays on behalf of the saints, because believers do not always know exactly what to pray for. Patrick uses this verse in order to interpret what he saw, and as a result is quite certain that the Spirit of God prayed within him with inexpressible groans.

The Spirit spoke to Patrick through his infallible Word. But, as we have seen in the preceding discussion of prayer and the Holy Spirit, it is also obvious that Patrick believed the Holy Spirit sometimes spoke to him in dreams.[28] Like others in the ancient church, Patrick was convinced that dreams were an authentic medium that the Spirit used to speak to the people of God.[29] Patrick refers to seven specific dream sequences in the *Confession*, and, apart from one of them, they are all clustered near the beginning of Patrick's account of his life.[30] All of Patrick's dreams relate to either issues of personal guidance, such as his call to mission in Ireland, or personal encouragement; none of them are employed to determine or set forth doctrine. In the medieval world, dreams and visions sometimes supplant God's Word as the main way he communicates with men and women. But such cannot be said of Patrick. As we have seen, he is deeply committed to the Word being the vehicle by which he obtains light and wisdom for his life. But he does conceive obviously of the Spirit as a living presence and person in his life, who has, in the course of his life and ministry, used dreams occasionally (if there are only seven such times in the course of fifty years, that really is an extremely small number) to encourage him and confirm courses of action.[31]

---

28. For a discussion of Patrick's dreams, see O'Donoghue, *Aristocracy of Soul*, p. 11-23.

29. For a detailed study of Patristic oneirology, see Lien-Yueh Wei, 'Doctrinalising Dreams: Patristic Views of the Nature of Dreams and Their Relation to Early Christian Doctrines' (PhD thesis, New College, University of Edinburgh, 2011).

30. *Confessions* 17–25 and 29.

31. For two helpful studies of Reformed perspectives on the matter of dreams and visions, see Christopher Bennett, 'The Puritans and the Direct Operations of Holy Spirit' in *Building on A Sure Foundation. Papers read at the 1994 Westminster Conference* ([London]: The Westminster Conference, 1994), pp. 108-22 and Garnet Howard Milne, *The Westminster Confession of Faith and the Cessation of Special Revelation* (Milton Keynes, England: Paternoster, 2007), *passim*.

The Spirit and Patrick's ministry

Patrick's call to ministry or personal drive to minister to others is marked by a sense of inadequacy. Patrick is not a trained thinker. He is unclear in his speech. He blushes as he writes, for his writings reveal a distinct lack of education. Pervasive in Patrick's two works is a 'strong sense of inadequacy and inferiority'.[32] This constant challenge, however, is more than met by the powerful ministry of the Holy Spirit. As Patrick says:

> As a youth, nay, almost as a boy not able to speak, I was taken captive, before I knew what to pursue and what to avoid. Hence to-day I blush and am afraid to reveal my lack of education; for I am unable to tell my story to those versed in the art of concise writing — in such a way, I mean, as my spirit and mind long to do, and so that the sense of my words expresses what I feel.

> But if indeed it had been given to me as it was given to others, then I would not be silent because of my desire of thanksgiving; and if perhaps some people think me arrogant for doing so in spite of my lack of knowledge and my slow tongue, it is, after all, written: 'The stammering tongues shall quickly learn to speak peace.'[33]

> How much more should we earnestly strive to do this, we, who are, so Scripture says, 'a letter of Christ' for salvation unto the utmost part of the earth, and, though not an eloquent one, yet 'written in your hearts, not with ink, but with the Spirit of the living God'[34]! And again the Spirit witnesses that even 'rusticity (*rusticationem*) was created by the Highest.'[35]

Despite the fact that Patrick's lack of learning prevents him from expressing himself as he desires, unlike some who were well versed in the art of rhetoric, the Holy Spirit has made Patrick 'a

---

32. R.P.C. Hanson, *The Life and Writings of the Historical Saint Patrick* (New York, NY: The Seabury Press, 1983), p. 37.

33. Isaiah 32:4

34. 2 Corinthians 3:3

35. Ecclesiasticus 7:16 (Old Latin version)

letter of Christ for salvation' to the Irish who live at 'the utmost part of the earth'. The Spirit has used Patrick despite his limitations in Latin to write the Gospel of salvation in their hearts. So Patrick can declare that the Spirit bears witness that even 'rusticity' has a place in the unfolding of God's plan in history. This final quote is from the apocryphal Ecclesiasticus, one of at least eight quotes from the Apocrypha (the other books cited are Tobit and the Wisdom of Solomon). The Latin word translated here 'rusticity' is *rusticatio*, which actually means 'farming' or 'farm operations'. Patrick has confused it (purposely?) with *rusticitas*, which means 'lack of sophistication'. The fact that Patrick quotes from the Apocrypha does not necessarily mean that he believes them to be on a par with the inspired Scriptures, any more than the citation of verses from the Assumption of Moses and 1 Enoch by Jude mean that he regarded them as inspired Scripture. Yet, Patrick's use of this text from Ecclesiasticus confirms for him that the Spirit does not only use those who are learned, but he even employs some like him, slow of speech and unlearned.

It is also the indwelling Holy Spirit, as a gift, who enables Patrick to stay focused on his ministry while undergoing adversity. The 'gift' of the Spirit had been bestowed on him during his captivity. In Patrick's Trinitarian rule of faith, as we have seen, the Holy Spirit is called the gift and pledge.[36] This salvation, brought by the indwelling Holy Spirit, keeps Patrick steadfast in his mission. For instance, Patrick recalls the friend, 'the face of Deisignatus', who was involved in bringing charges against Patrick.[37] These had to do with Patrick's confession of a certain sin done by him prior to his conversion.[38] Stopping his recollection of this traumatic event by saying 'enough of this', Patrick was able to continue his mission because of the indwelling Spirit: 'Enough of this. I must

---

36. *Confession* 4.

37. *Confession* 29, trans. Bieler, p. 30.

38. *Confession* 27.

not, however, hide God's gift which he bestowed upon me in the
land of my captivity; because then I earnestly sought him, and
there I found him, and he saved me from all evil because – so
I believe – of his Spirit that dwells in me.'[39]

While undergoing hardship in Ireland, Patrick finds himself
'bound by the Spirit' to stay there. The hardship Patrick particularly recalls is not the hardship of persecution or famine or
distress. Rather, Patrick longs to see the once familiar faces of
his countrymen, his parents, and the saints residing in Britain.
Patrick feels the travail of loneliness.

> Wherefore, then, even if I wished to leave them and go to Brit-
> ain – and how I would have loved to go to my country and my
> parents, and also to Gaul in order to visit the brethren and to
> see the face of the saints of my Lord! God knows that I much
> desired it; but I am bound by the Spirit, who gives evidence
> against me if I do this, telling me that I shall be guilty; and I am
> afraid of losing the labour which I have begun – nay, not I, but
> Christ the Lord who bade me come here and stay with them for
> the rest of my life, if the Lord will, and will guard me from every
> evil way that I may not sin before Him.[40]

Despite his lack of family, the Spirit sustained him in the midst of
his ministry in Ireland. It is quite natural to desire to see the face
of a familiar family member or beloved saint, but because Patrick
was bound by the Spirit of God, he persevered. Moreover, if he
were to go to Britain, he feared losing his ministry, for Patrick
recognized that it was Christ the Lord who had led him to come
to Ireland in the first place.

Patrick's *Letter to the Soldiers of Coroticus* further reiterates this
idea. He informs them he has come to Ireland not according to
his flesh, meaning selfish or personal motivations, but according
to God. 'I am bound by the Spirit,' Patrick says once more, 'not
to see any of my kinsfolk.'[41]

---

39. *Confession* 33, trans. Bieler, p. 31, altered.

40. *Confession* 43, trans. Bieler, p. 35.

41. *Letter to the Soldiers of Coroticus* 10, trans. Bieler, p. 43.

Is it of my own doing that I have holy mercy on the people who once took me captive and made away with the servants and maids of my father's house? I was freeborn according to the flesh. I am the son of a Decurion. But I sold my noble rank – I am neither ashamed nor sorry – for the good of others. Thus I am a servant in Christ to a foreign nation for the unspeakable glory of life everlasting which is in Christ Jesus our Lord.[42]

The Spirit has bound Patrick to forsake all in order to spread the name of God to a foreign nation. His noble birth is now of no avail; his transformed convictions oblige Patrick to stay in Ireland as a servant of Christ.

The Holy Spirit, then, plays an absolutely vital role in enabling Patrick to stay faithful to the call of missions. The Spirit enables him to persevere in prayer, to remain faithful despite his feelings of utter inadequacy, and to stay in Ireland no matter the cost. The Spirit has indeed woven himself into the entire fabric of Patrick's ministry; without him he could have done nothing.

'I am a bishop'

Despite the way pictorial renditions and sculpted depictions of Patrick err by usually portraying him in the garb of a medieval ecclesiastic, these visual images do retain one key note from the life of the historical Patrick: he was a missionary bishop. In his letter to the soldiers of the war chief Coroticus, Patrick wastes no time at the beginning of the letter to emphasize his authority: 'I, Patrick, a sinner, unlearned, ... affirm that I am a bishop. Most assuredly I believe that what I am I have received from God.'[43] Patrick mentions his episcopacy on only two other occasions.

---

42. *Letter to the Soldiers of Coroticus* 10, trans. Bieler, pp. 43-4.
43. *Letter to the Soldiers of Coroticus* 1, trans. Bieler, p. 41, altered.

In *Confession* 32 he recalls that a close friend had told him that he believed he 'should be raised to the rank of bishop'.[44] It was this very same friend who failed to defend him when serious charges regarding money were levelled against him by leaders and elders in the British church.[45] The third reference to his ministry as a bishop comes at the beginning of the section of the *Confession* where Patrick replies to the charges brought against him. There he mentions his 'hard work as a bishop' (*laboriosum episcopatum*).[46] From Patrick's own writings, this hard work would undoubtedly have involved preaching and baptizing new converts, as well as the choosing, discipling, and appointment of elders.[47] He does not mention the presence of any other bishops in Ireland, though there are accounts of another bishop, a certain Palladius, preceding him.[48] Nor does Patrick ever mention that he was sent by the Bishop of Rome to Ireland, which, if that had been the case, he might have used in his defence over the charges raised against him near the close of his life.[49]

By Patrick's day, bishops had become powerful figures in the Roman world.[50] In addition to their responsibilities

---

44. *Confession* 32, trans. Bieler, p. 30.

45. See above, Chapter 3.

46. I owe this translation to Padraig McCarthy, trans., *My Name is Patrick. St Patrick's Confessio* (Dublin: Royal Irish Academy, 2011), p. 13.

47. For Patrick as a preacher, see *Confession* 11, 14, 34, 47, 58; *Letter to the Soldiers of Coroticus* 1; for his baptizing new believers, see *Confession* 38, 50, 51; *Letter to the Soldiers of Coroticus* 2–3; and for his appointing elders, see *Confession* 38, 40, 51.

48. On Palladius, see R.P.C. Hanson, *Saint Patrick: His Origins and Career* (Oxford: Clarendon Press, 1968), pp. 52-6, 192-5. For an early text that indicates Palladius was sent by the Bishop of Rome, see Muirchú, *Life* 1.8, trans. Ludwig Bieler, *The Patrician Texts in the Book of Armagh* (Dublin: The Dublin Institute for Advanced Studies, 1979), p. 73.

49. F.R. Montgomery Hitchcock, *St Patrick and his Gallic Friends* (London: Society for Promoting Christian Knowledge, 1916), pp. 19, 25-6.

50. See the very helpful study of the early Christian bishop by Henry Chadwick, 'The Role of the Christian Bishop in Ancient Society' in his *Heresy and Orthodoxy in the Early Church* (Aldershot, Hampshire: Variorum, 1991), no. III, pp. 1-14. The following outline of episcopal duties is dependent on Chadwick.

Palladius

According to Prosper of Aquitaine, in his timeline of the fifth century, in 431, 'Palladius, having been ordained by Pope Celestine, was sent to the Irish believers in Christ as their first bishop.' This brief sentence raises a number of important questions: Who was Palladius? Where did these Irish believers come from? How many of them were there? How had they come to faith in Christ? And if Palladius preceded Patrick, why is it Patrick who is remembered as the apostle to the Irish? Given the proximity of Ireland to Britain and the commerce that went back and forth between the two, it is not surprising that Christianity had found a foothold in Ireland – and that probably through the witness of merchants and slaves – before Patrick came back as an evangelist. But given the fact that Patrick makes no mention of believers before his evangelistic mission, there could not have been many of them. Patrick's ministry was also mostly restricted to the northern half of the island. These believers may well have been in the south-east, in Leinster. Palladius had served as a deacon in the church at Rome before becoming a bishop. His mission to Ireland was not remembered and cannot have been a lengthy one. It is also noteworthy that Palladius's mission was not explicitly missional – it was intended to provide spiritual nurture for those who were already believers. Patrick's ministry was quite different: from the start it sought to convert Irish unbelievers.

of teaching, preaching, and leading in worship, they were expected to provide hospitality to travellers and ensure there was provision for the poor. They also served as judges in legal matters involving the Christian community. As Henry Chadwick has noted: judicial 'arbitrations became a major preoccupation of bishops'.[51] They would even help negotiate the release of prisoners of war and some served sometimes as ambassadors between Rome and her 'barbarian' neighbours. The danger of their misuse of this authority and power is evident in what Patrick's older contemporary, the monastic leader John Cassian (c. 360–c. 435), once termed 'an old saying

51. Chadwick, 'Role of the Christian Bishop', p. 6.

of the fathers', namely, 'A monk must by all means flee from women and bishops'![52]

Patrick's episcopate, of course, was exercised within ancient Irish society, which was a very different social and cultural context than that of the Roman Empire, as we have seen in previous chapters. As such, a number of the episcopal roles exercised by bishops within the Empire seem to have no parallel in his ministry. For instance, there is no indication at all that Patrick ever exercised any judicial authority. On the other hand, his letter to Coroticus echoes the way ancient bishops did help secure the release of those taken captive by peoples outside of the Roman Empire. In fact, Patrick explicitly notes that it was 'the custom of the Roman Christians of Gaul ... [to] send holy and able men to the Franks and other peoples ... to ransom baptized captives'.[53] One can thus hear and see Patrick's episcopal authority at work when he tells Coroticus and his men that because of what they have done they are 'fellow citizens of the demons' and 'far from the love of God'.[54] They are nothing less than 'rebels against Christ' and 'enemies of me and of Christ my God, for whom I am an ambassador'.[55] And as the Lord's spokesperson, Patrick, along with other bishops – he calls them 'priests (*sacerdotes*)' at this point – has been given what he calls 'the highest power, one that is divine and truly distinguished (*summam divinam sublimam potestatem*), that those whom they bind on earth are bound in heaven'.[56] Patrick clearly understands Christ's words in Matthew 16:19 to apply to the bishops of the church: it is they who have the power to receive people into the church and it is they who have the power to excommunicate them. As Ludwig

---

52. *The Institutes* 11.18, trans. Boniface Ramsey, *John Cassian: The Institutes* (Ancient Christian Writers, no.58; New York, NY/Mahwah, NJ: Newman Press, 2000), p. 247.

53. *Letter to the Soldiers of Coroticus* 14, trans. Bieler, p. 45, altered.

54. *Letter to the Soldiers of Coroticus* 2 and 12, trans. Bieler, pp. 41 and 44.

55. *Letter to the Soldiers of Coroticus* 19 and 5, trans. Bieler, pp. 46 and 42, altered.

56. *Letter to the Soldiers of Coroticus* 6, trans. Bieler, p. 42, altered.

Bieler has pointed out, Patrick's words also echo a statement from the North African bishop, Cyprian (c. 200–258), whose writings were so influential in shaping the Latin-speaking tradition of thought about the church. In a letter written in 252, Cyprian referred to the power given to bishops to govern the church as 'truly distinguished and divine (*sublimi ac divina potestate*)'.[57] Whether or not Patrick knows this actual letter of the African bishop – and I am personally dubious that he did – Patrick clearly stands in the Cyprianic tradition with regard to the authority of the bishop. In such a tradition, the bishop was the central authority in the church, an authority established by Christ's words in Matthew 16:18-19, such that Cyprian could actually affirm that 'the church is established upon the bishops'.[58]

As a bishop, Patrick has the authority to excommunicate Coroticus — hence his blistering letter to the warlord. Where did that authority come from? For Patrick, it is clear that it is grounded in Christ's words in Matthew 16. He also makes it clear that with regard to himself, his being a bishop is all of God's grace. As he stated in the passage cited above from the opening lines of the letter to Coroticus's men: 'I, Patrick ... affirm that I am a bishop. Most assuredly I believe that what I am I have received from God.'[59] Thus, the Holy Spirit's making him a missionary to the Irish also entailed the call to be a bishop. Like his episcopal predecessor Cyprian, Patrick seems to have had no doubts that bishops were central to the Spirit's ordering of the Church.

---

57. Cyprian, *Letter* 59.2, ed. William Hartel, *S. Thasci Caecili Cypriani Opera Omnia* (Corpus Scriptorum Ecclesiasticorum Latinorum, vol.3/1; Vienna, 1868), p. 667, lines 14-15, trans. Michael A. G. Haykin. See Bieler, *The Works of St Patrick, St Secundinus*, p. 91, n. 12.

58. *Letter* 33.1, ed. Hartel, *S. Thasci Caecili Cypriani Opera Omnia*, p. 566.

59. *Letter to the Soldiers of Coroticus* 1, trans. Bieler, p. 41, altered.

5

AN EVANGELICAL REFLECTS ON PATRICK

E.A. Thompson has rightly noted that Patrick's 'character is complex and of the utmost fascination'.[1] My own fascination with Patrick began quite early in my studies of the ancient church. Initially, I suspect I was drawn to him because of my Irish ancestry. But in time, his rich Trinitarianism and zeal for missions, his biblicism and dependence on the Spirit exercised their own pull on my heart and mind. Since 1989 I have written a number of pieces on Patrick.[2] In this book-length essay, however, I have not only sought to bring together the various strands of all that I have written about Patrick, but I have also expanded this material considerably so that readers today might see the implications of his life and thought for contemporary Evangelicalism.

1. 'Reviews', *Britannia*, 11 (1980), p. 440.

2. See '"Bound by the Spirit": An Appreciation of Patrick' in Michael A.G. Haykin, ed., *For A Testimony [Mark 13:9]. Essays in Honour of John H. Wilson* (Toronto, ON: Central Baptist Seminary and Bible College, 1989), pp. 45-61; 'Patrick of Ireland (c. 390–c. 460)' in Glen G. Scorgie, Simon Chan, Gordon T. Smith, and James D. Smith III, eds., *Zondervan Dictionary of Christian Spirituality* (Grand Rapids, MI: Zondervan, 2011), pp. 656-7; 'Patrick: Inspiration for the Mission of William Carey and his Friends', *The Banner of Truth*, 594 (March 2013), pp. 5-8. See also the chapters on Patrick in *Defence of the Truth: Contending for the truth yesterday and today* (Darlington, Co. Durham: Evangelical Press, 2004) and *Rediscovering the Church Fathers: Who They Were and How They Shaped the Church* (Wheaton, IL: Crossway, 2011).

It would be both wrong and anachronistic to describe Patrick as an Evangelical. His encouragement of monasticism, for example, hardly squares with Evangelical piety.[3] His devotion to the Trinity, however, has much to teach Evangelicals, far too many of whom seem to have forgotten the absolute necessity of being Trinitarian in teaching and worship. His zeal for missions and the salvation of the lost is not only inspiring, but deeply convicting. Also, he is into missions for all of the right reasons: the glory of God; his love for the lost, in this case, the Irish, and his concern for their salvation; the duty he owes to God's call on his own life; and obedience of the Scriptural mandate to take the gospel to the ends of the earth. Then, there is his bibliocentrism: whether he had read many other books or not, he leaves us with the overwhelming impression that only one book supremely matters, and that is the Bible. He is not afraid to find truth in other sources – all truth is God's truth – but in the final analysis, it is Scripture that guides him. Finally, I love his dependence on the Spirit. While his thought and expression are indeed shaped by God's infallible Word, he sought in all integrity to listen to the Spirit in his daily life and so find that much-needed balance of Word and Spirit that we all require in our day.[4] Most importantly in this regard, because of his own weaknesses, Patrick knew that the Spirit's work in us is a humbling work, showing us that all in the Christian life is of pure grace: a truly Evangelical note – 'if I have achieved or shown any small success according to God's pleasure, ... it was the gift of God.'[5]

---

3. See *Confession* 41–42, 49; *Letter to the Soldiers of Coroticus* 12. Christine Mohrmann [*The Latin of Saint Patrick* (Dublin: Dublin Institute for Advanced Studies, 1961), p. 26] is not convinced that 'the Irish church of his [i.e. Patrick's] time was characterized by monasticism'.

4. See especially the helpful essay on this topic by Christopher Bennett, 'The Puritans and the Direct Operations of Holy Spirit' in *Building on A Sure Foundation. Papers read at the 1994 Westminster Conference* ([London]: The Westminster Conference, 1994), pp. 108-22.

5. *Confession* 62, trans. R.P.C. Hanson, *The Life and Writings of the Historical Saint Patrick* (New York, NY: The Seabury Press, 1983), p. 124.

FURTHER READING

M.W. Barley and R.P.C. Hanson, eds., *Christianity in Britain, 300–700*. [Leicester]: Leicester University Press, 1968.
This book is a collection of essays by several scholars on a variety of subjects pertaining to the British Church. Several notable Patrician scholars make contributions to the work, including Ludwig Bieler, R.P.C. Hanson, and E.A. Thompson. Of particular importance is Bieler's chapter that tackles Patrick's place within the larger context of the British church. Also noteworthy is Bieler's account of Patrick's mission to Ireland which, contrary to Hanson, Bieler argues is to be regarded as one that originated in Gaul rather than Britain.

J.B. Bury, *The Life of St Patrick and His Place in History*. London: Macmillan and Co., 1905.
First published in 1905 and reprinted in the late 1990s, Bury's text was foundational to later Patrician studies. Offering a survey of Patrick's life and his historical context, Bury's work relied upon the later medieval biographies. While this led to many of his conclusions being challenged by later historians such as R.P.C. Hanson, Bury's work is nonetheless beneficial to students of Patrick, early British Christianity, and the history of Patrician scholarship.

Liam de Paor, *Saint Patrick's World: The Christian Culture of Ireland's Apostolic Age.* **Dublin: Four Courts Press, 1996.**
As the title suggests, Liam de Paor's work seeks to place Patrick in the larger context of the fifth-century Celtic world. The first part of the book includes short chapters on various topics including the arrival of Christianity to Britain, the British Church, Ireland in the fifth-century, and also a chapter on the contribution of women to the early Irish Church. Part two not only includes de Paor's translations of Patrick's two surviving works, but also a wide range of primary source material such as later medieval biographies of Patrick, annals that mention Patrick (or figures associated with him), and several biographies of other prominent Irish figures such as Columbanus. While the usefulness of these latter works in reconstructing Patrick's life is questionable, they will nevertheless be of interest to students of Patrick.

Máire de Paor, *Patrick, the Pilgrim Apostle of Ireland.* **New York, NY: Regan Books, 1998.**
Máire de Paor's work challenges the often-held notion that Patrick was an ignoramus who struggled to express himself in Latin. De Paor seeks to demonstrate that both Patrick's *Confession* and *Epistle* reveal him to have had a mastery of the Scriptures and great sophistication as a writer. Although de Paor includes a brief introduction that discusses some of the historical problems surrounding the details of Patrick's life, the bulk of the work is comprised of an in-depth analysis of Patrick's use of Scriptural references, the literary structure of his writings, and his theology. Also included are the Latin texts of Patrick's works.

Philip Freeman, *St Patrick of Ireland: A Biography.* **New York, NY: Simon & Schuster, 2004.**
This study of Patrick's life by Philip Freeman, professor of Classics at Washington University, St Louis, is an extremely well told account. Freeman rightly assumes that the whole of what we can know about the historical Patrick must begin with his two

undoubted writings: *The Confession* and his *Letter to the Soldiers of Coroticus*. Freeman includes translations of these two works in an epilogue (pp. 169-93). To someone used to a standard translation of these two works, like that of Ludwig Bieler, Freeman's translation might seem somewhat loose and too colloquial. On the other hand, his translation does have the advantage of making Patrick and his world come alive.

R.P.C. Hanson, *The Life and Writings of the Historical Saint Patrick*. New York, NY: Seabury Press, 1983.

This short work is the perfect starting point for newcomers to studies of Patrick. The first part of Hanson's work is an introduction that presents readers with the challenges faced by historians when reconstructing Patrick's life, including discussions on dating Patrick's life, the location of his birthplace, his education, his career in Ireland, and an assessment of the primary sources available to historians today. The second part of the book consists of Hanson's own translations of Patrick's writings that are supplemented with a brief chapter-by-chapter commentary that primarily highlights the historical issues raised in each passage.

R.P.C. Hanson, *Saint Patrick: His Origins and Career*. Oxford: Clarendon Press, 1968.

Readers of Hanson's *The Life and Writings of the Historical Saint Patrick* will likely be interested in this work, which offers a more in-depth treatment of the various historical problems concerning Patrick's life. Interacting with the works of other notable Patrician scholars, Hanson begins with a discussion of the fifth-century British church and proceeds to cover topics ranging from the date of Patrick's life and career, his education, and his use of Latin. Particularly helpful is Hanson's extensive assessment of sources outside of Patrick's own writings that have been used to reconstruct Patrick's life. These sources, including later medieval biographies and annals, are ultimately judged by Hanson to be historically unreliable.

John T. McNeill, *The Celtic Churches: A History* A.D. *200 to 1200.* **Chicago, IL/London: University of Chicago Press, 1974.**
While the focus of this fine work is not primarily concerned with Patrick, McNeill's sweeping survey of the Celtic church, from its roots during the Roman Empire to the end of the Middle Ages, is nonetheless valuable in placing Patrick in the larger context of the Celtic church and his contribution to it.

Saint Patrick's Confessio **(http://www.confessio.ie; accessed November 3, 2013).**
Considering many materials on Patrick can be hard to come by, those interested in Patrick, whether newcomers or scholars, will find this website extremely valuable. The website contains a treasure trove of materials relating to Patrick that ranges from primary texts translated into several languages to viewable digital images of original medieval documents such as the *Book of Armagh*, which contains, among other things, a version of Patrick's *Confession*. Latin texts are available, notably Ludwig Bieler's canonical edition which allows users to consult his commentary, variant readings, and biblical references found in Patrick's works. Also of note is the extensive bibliography that lists many primary sources, books, and scholarly articles pertaining to Patrick and the Irish church, several of which are accessible online.

E.A. Thompson, *Who Was Saint Patrick?* **Woodbridge, Suffolk: Boydell Press, 1985.**
In his book, Thompson explores in depth the historical problems that present themselves in Patrick's works. Thompson works through the *Confession* and critically examines nearly every major event described by Patrick, including his birthplace and dates, his enslavement as a young boy, and his mission to Ireland.

Also available in the Early Church Fathers *series...*

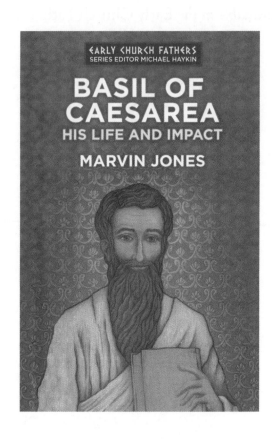

EARLY CHURCH FATHERS
SERIES EDITOR MICHAEL HAYKIN

BASIL OF CAESAREA
HIS LIFE AND IMPACT

MARVIN JONES

ISBN 978-1-78191-302-4

BASIL OF CAESAREA

MARVIN JONES

Basil of Caesarea (A.D. 329-379) was a Greek Bishop in what is now Turkey. A thoughtful theologian, he was instrumental in the formation of the Nicene Creed. He fought a growing heresy, Arianism, that had found converts, including those in high positions of state. In the face of such a threat he showed courage, wisdom and complete confidence in God that we would do well to emulate today.

Marvin Jones is Chair of the Christian Studies Department and Assistant Professor of Church History and Theology at Louisiana College in Pineville, Louisiana. He holds degrees from Southeastern Baptist Theological Seminary, Dallas Theological Seminary and the University of South Africa.

Also available from Christian Focus...

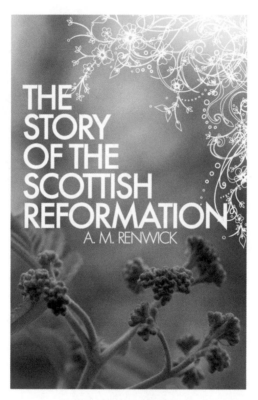

THE
STORY
OF THE
SCOTTISH
REFORMATION
A. M. RENWICK

978-1-84550-598-1

THE STORY OF THE SCOTTISH REFORMATION

A.M RENWICK

The Reformation had a radical effect on Scotland not just spiritually but also politically and socially. Given its spiritual decadence in the lead up to this, it was in much need of reformation. A contributor to that success was the old Celtic Church who revered the Bible as the supreme standard and hence placed an emphasis on the preaching of the Word. Renwick considers the character and the experiences of the leader of the Scottish Reformation John Knox. Secularly it was to have an influence on the Scottish Parliament e.g. the importance of education for all as a result of the principles they had established. It also considers the protagonists of the reformation such as the nobles and the place of Mary of Lorraine, the Queen Mother, and Queen Mary. As well as looking at the Scottish Reformation it gives its historical context not forgetting what was happening elsewhere. It is clear that for those who were involved in the Scottish Reformation it was costly but they considered it important to defend the reformed faith. An opportunity to read of lives that were transformed as they became convicted of the gospel truth which in turn led them to serve God.

I am delighted to see this classic study of the Scottish Reformation by Prof. Renwick come back into print...It is written with the two qualities Calvin desired for his own literary productions: clarity and brevity.

Douglas F. Kelly
Richard Jordan Professor of Theology
Reformed Theological Seminary, Charlotte, North Carolina

Dr A. M. Renwick was professor of Church History at the Free Church of Scotland College in Edinburgh.

A Heart for Mission

Five Pioneer Thinkers

Jonathan Edwards, Cotton Mather, Richard Baxter,
Jan Amos Comenius, Count Zinzendorf

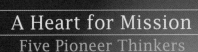

Ron Davies

978-1-85792-233-2

A HEART FOR MISSION

RON DAVIES

Most commentators agree that the Protestant Missionary effort really got under way in the late eighteenth century with the formation of the Baptist Missionary Society. Bearing in mind that the Reformation began in the early sixteenth century the obvious question that arises is 'Why did it take Protestants nearly three centuries to act on Jesus' Great Commission mandate?'

This book goes some of the way to explaining why. We are introduced to five Protestant, Christian thinkers who had a mind for mission, long before the Protestant World as a whole became aware of the need. From the celebrated Jonathan Edwards to the comparatively unknown Jan Amos Comenius, we see how these five men were ahead of their time. They influenced thinking about mission and their comments ultimately led to the missionary explosion which began at the end of the eighteenth century and which carries on to the present day.

Ron Davies' book ...treats us to brief biographical backgrounds and then proceeds to show their passion for international cross-cultural mission. May this book be used of God to move today's church to a greater self-sacrifice for the spread of the good news of Jesus Christ worldwide.

Martin Goldsmith,
Author and former OMF Missionary in Asia

Ron Davies has lectured at All Nations Christian College since 1964 and has been a visiting lecturer at several seminaries in Eastern Europe and elsewhere. He also spent four years in the early nineties as an Adjunct Professor at Fuller Theological Seminary. He has made many contributions to a wide range of periodicals and journals.

Christian Focus Publications

Our mission statement –

STAYING FAITHFUL

In dependence upon God we seek to impact the world through literature faithful to His infallible Word, the Bible. Our aim is to ensure that the Lord Jesus Christ is presented as the only hope to obtain forgiveness of sin, live a useful life and look forward to heaven with Him.

Our Books are published in four imprints:

CHRISTIAN
FOCUS

popular works including biographies, commentaries, basic doctrine and Christian living.

CHRISTIAN
HERITAGE

books representing some of the best material from the rich heritage of the church.

MENTOR

books written at a level suitable for Bible College and seminary students, pastors, and other serious readers. The imprint includes commentaries, doctrinal studies, examination of current issues and church history.

CF4•K

children's books for quality Bible teaching and for all age groups: Sunday school curriculum, puzzle and activity books; personal and family devotional titles, biographies and inspirational stories – Because you are never too young to know Jesus!

Christian Focus Publications Ltd,
Geanies House, Fearn, Ross-shire,
IV20 1TW, Scotland, United Kingdom.
www.christianfocus.com